THE MANHATTAN PROJECT

THE MANHATTAN PROJECT

Daniel Cohen

Twenty-First Century Books
Brookfield, Connecticut

Photographs courtesy of Science Source/Photo Researchers: pp. 12 (Mehau Kulyk/Science Photo Library), 32 (Los Alamos National Laboratory/Mark Marten), 45 (Los Alamos National Laboratory/Science Photo Library), 79 (Los Alamos National Laboratory/Mark Marten), 103 (U.S. Air Force/Science Photo Library); AP/Wide World Photos: pp. 17 (top), 68, 76, 89; UPI/Corbis-Bettmann: pp. 17 (bottom), 50, 59, 81, 91; Corbis-Bettmann: pp. 26, 106; © Gamma Liaison: p. 35 (Eric Brissaud/Los Alamos National Laboratory); Los Alamos National Laboratory: p. 43; National Security Agency/Central Intelligence Agency: p. 93; The Chicago *Sun-Times* © 1998: p. 113 (Rich Hein)

Library of Congress Cataloging-in-Publication Data
Cohen, Daniel, 1936–
The Manhattan Project / Daniel Cohen.
p.   cm.
Includes bibliographical references and index.
Summary: Discusses the personalities and events involved in the research, development, and detonation of the atomic bombs built by the United States in the 1940s.
ISBN 0-7613-0359-6 (lib. bdg.)
1. Atomic bomb—United States—History—Juvenile literature. 2. Manhattan Project (U.S.)—History—Juvenile literature. [1. Manhattan Project (U.S.) — History. 2. Atomic bomb—History.] I. Title.
QC773.3.U5C64   1999
355.8'25119—dc21   98-44499   CIP   AC

Published by Twenty-First Century Books
A Division of The Millbrook Press
2 Old New Milford Road, Brookfield, Connecticut 06804
www.millbrookpress.com

Contents

Introduction
TRINITY—JULY 16, 1945
9

Chapter One
THE EINSTEIN LETTER
13

Chapter Two
**"THE ITALIAN NAVIGATOR
HAS JUST LANDED"**
21

Chapter Three
THE ODD COUPLE
30

Chapter Four
LOS ALAMOS
40

Chapter Five
THE GERMAN BOMB PROJECT
52

Chapter Six
THE ROAD TO TRINITY
63

Chapter Seven
TESTING "THE GADGET"
71

Chapter Eight
SPIES
84

Chapter Nine
AFTER TRINITY
99

Chapter Ten
THE DOOMSDAY CLOCK
110

Chronology
117

Notes
119

Bibliography
122

Index
125

THE MANHATTAN PROJECT

TRINITY
July 16, 1945

On MONDAY, JULY 16, 1945, at 5:29 A.M., Mountain War Time, there was an explosion in the northwest corner of the Alamogordo Bombing Range (known as the Trinity site) that changed the world forever.

Years later physicist Isidore I. Rabi, who was at Base Camp 10 miles (16 kilometers) from the blast, recalled the event:

"We were lying there, very tense, in the early dawn, and there were just a few streaks of gold in the east; you could see your neighbor very dimly. Those ten seconds were the longest I ever experienced. Suddenly, there was an enormous flash of light, the brightest light I have ever seen or that I think anyone has ever seen. It blasted; it pounced; it bored its way right through you. It was a vision which was seen with more than the eye. It was seen to last forever. You would wish it would stop; altogether it lasted about two seconds. Finally it was over, diminishing, and we looked toward the place where the bomb had been; there was an enormous ball of fire which grew and grew and it rolled as it grew; it went up into the air in yellow flashes and into scarlet and green. It looked menacing. It seemed to come toward one.

"A new thing had been born; a new control; a new understanding of man, which man had acquired over nature."[1]

Another physicist at Base Camp, Emilio Segre, had visions of the apocalypse:

"The most striking impression was that of an overwhelmingly bright light. . . . I was flabbergasted by the new spectacle. We saw the whole sky flash with unbelievable brightness in spite of the very dark glasses we wore. . . . I believe that for a moment I thought the explosion might set fire to the atmosphere and thus finish the earth, even though I knew this was not possible."[2]

Enrico Fermi had prepared an experiment to determine the strength of the bomb. Seconds before the bomb exploded, Fermi began tearing up paper into small pieces. After he saw the flash he dropped the paper from his hand, and when the blast wave hit he measured how far it carried them.

"Since at the time there was no wind, I could observe very distinctly and actually measure the displacement of the pieces of paper that were in the process of falling while the blast was passing."

The paper traveled about 8 feet (2½ meters). He then pulled out his slide rule and calculated that the energy of the explosion was in the range of 10,000 tons of TNT. Later instrument readings were to show that the yield of the Trinity device was actually closer to 19,000 to 20,000 tons (19 or 20 kilotons). "He was so profoundly absorbed in his bits of paper," said his wife, Laura Fermi, "that he was not aware of the tremendous noise."

General Leslie Groves, who had been the top military man on the project that produced the bomb, had a far more mundane reaction. He recalled thinking about the man who had crossed Niagara Falls on a tightrope. " . . . only to me the tightrope had lasted almost three years, and of my repeated, confident-appearing assurances that such a thing was possible and we would do it." Immediately after the historic explosion General Groves shook hands with some of his colleagues.

All of those at the site of the explosion knew what had happened. But hundreds of others saw the explosion and had no idea what it was. Some thought it was a meteor; others thought it was an airplane crash or even a Japanese bombing.

Mrs. H. W. Wieselman had just driven across the Arizona–New Mexico line, en route from California, when she saw it. She remembered:

"We had just left Safford, and it was still dark. Suddenly the tops of high mountains by which we were passing were lighted up by a reddish, orange light.

"The surrounding countryside was illuminated like daylight for about three seconds.

"Then it was dark again.

"The experience scared me. It was just like the sun had come up and suddenly gone down again."[3]

Probably the most remarkable statement about the blast came from Georgia Green of Socorro, New Mexico. She was a University of New Mexico music student who was being driven up to Albuquerque for her morning class by her brother-in-law. "What's that?" she asked as the light from Trinity reached her eyes. Georgia Green was blind, though she could detect very strong light.

The classic Bohr Model showing atomic structure. The orbits of the electrons around a central nucleus is now thought to be not as rigidly symmetrical as Bohr proposed. This concept predates the Quantum theory and shows the electrons in a well-defined circular orbit.

Chapter 1

THE EINSTEIN LETTER

As the 20th century dawned, the field of theoretical physics was undergoing a remarkable revolution. Starting with the discovery of X rays in 1895 by Wilhelm Roentgen, discoveries and radical new theories about the basic physical nature of the universe seemed to come tumbling out of the physicists' laboratories one after the other.

In 1902 the New Zealand–born scientist Ernest Rutherford, who is known as "the father of the nuclear age," began a series of experiments that were to reveal the nature of the atom itself. Building on Rutherford's discoveries, Danish physicist Niels Bohr developed the model of the structure of the atom, the nucleus surrounded by orbiting electrons, which is still familiar to us today.

During this same period, Albert Einstein conceived what is undoubtedly the most famous equation in all history $E=mc^2$: energy equals mass times the speed of light squared.

In 1938, German scientists discovered that if you bombarded the element uranium with neutrons, you could literally split the nucleus of an atom. They borrowed a term from biology and called the process nuclear "fission," or splitting. Within months scientists all over the world had repeated and refined the experiment.

In many respects the world of theoretical physics was an international or at least a European world. There were physicists in America, Japan, and elsewhere, but the major work was being done at universities in Cambridge, Rome, Berlin, and other European centers. The physicists all knew one another. They exchanged ideas and traveled freely back and forth. All that was about to change. The triumph of fascism in Hungary and Italy and of Nazism in Germany shattered the international community of scientists, forcing them to keep their discoveries within their own geographical or political borders.

During the late 1930s and early 1940s large numbers of scientists who were Jewish, and others who hated and feared the ideologies that had taken over their native lands, fled into exile. A significant percentage of them found refuge in the United States. The most famous of these émigrés was Albert Einstein, who settled at Princeton University.

Up to this point if they thought about it at all, the general public regarded theoretical physics as a strange, esoteric practice, rather like the attitude toward stellar astronomy today. It was all very interesting, but highly speculative and not the sort of thing that was going to have any effect on people's lives.

The physicists, however, thought differently. They knew that "splitting the atom," nuclear fission, could potentially release enormous amounts of energy. The splitting of one atom would result in its giving off particles that would split two other atoms, and so on. If billions of atoms fissioned in a chain reaction, powerful bombs might be created. In theory at least, this process could be used to create a weapon of almost unimaginable power. Since much of the work on nuclear fission had been done in Germany, German scientists certainly knew about this possibility. Yet almost no one in the United States seemed to take the potential development of a nuclear bomb very seriously.

Among the physicists none saw the possibility of using nuclear energy to create a superweapon more clearly than Hungarian-born Leo Szilard. He enlisted the cooperation of two Hungarian compatriots, Eugene Wigner and Edward Teller.

"The Hungarian conspiracy," as the trio was later called, became convinced that not only was the development of a nuclear weapon possible, but that the German government was almost certainly already doing research on such a weapon. The thought that Hitler might be the first to gain control of a weapon of enormous destructive potential power was terrifying to them. They decided that the administration of President Franklin D. Roosevelt must somehow be made aware of the danger, and the United States must begin its own atomic research project.

But how was this to be done? Though the three men, particularly Szilard, were well known in scientific circles it is doubtful if President Roosevelt had ever heard of them. The possibility that any of them would ever be able to get a private meeting with the president, much less get him to listen to their suggestions, which to the nonscientist would have sounded quite fantastic, was virtually nil.

But there was one man whose name Roosevelt certainly would have known, and whose lightest word on a matter of science would be taken seriously by any educated person— that was Albert Einstein.

Szilard was an old friend of Einstein's. He found out that Einstein was spending the summer in a house on Long Island, and he made an appointment to see him. Szilard didn't own a car and had never learned to drive. On the morning of Sunday, July 16, 1939, Wigner picked him up, and they drove out to Long Island.

They couldn't locate the address they had been given, but when they asked a boy where Professor Einstein lived, the cottage was pointed out to them immediately. Everyone knew Einstein: he personified science for laypeople.

The great man greeted them wearing an undershirt and rolled-up pants. Always informal in his dress, on vacation Einstein was more informal than ever. Szilard explained to Einstein how a chain reaction might be created. Einstein was quite surprised. *"Daran habe ich gar nicht gedacht!"* ("I never thought of that!") he exclaimed. But he grasped the possibility immediately and agreed to do anything he could to bring the dangers to the attention of the government.

Years later Szilard wrote: "[Einstein] was willing to assume responsibility for sounding the alarm even though it was quite possible that the alarm might prove to be a false alarm. The one thing most scientists are really afraid of is to make fools of themselves. Einstein was free from such a fear and this above all is what made his position unique on this occasion."[1]

As the plan finally evolved, Einstein was to write a letter to President Franklin D. Roosevelt about the possibilities and dangers of atomic weapons, and the letter would be taken to the president by Alexander Sachs, an economist and longtime friend of Roosevelt's.

It wasn't easy to get an appointment with Roosevelt in the late summer of 1939. Hitler had invaded Poland, and

Albert Einstein, right, waiting to give a speech in May 1940, in which he said that the supposedly exact science of physics was in about as chaotic condition as the situation in Europe. In addressing the American Scientific Congress he said that physicists "have to admit that we do not possess any general theoretical basis for physics which can be regarded as its logical foundation."

Dr. Leo Szilard in 1945, testifying before the Atomic Energy Committee that unnecessary military secrecy delayed development of the atomic bomb by more than a year.

the war in Europe had begun in earnest. Though the United States was not yet a participant in the war, the president certainly had his plate full, and even his old friend Sachs had great difficulty getting the appointment. Szilard and Wigner began to despair and started trying to think of other ways to reach the president.

Finally on October 11, after convincing Roosevelt's aides that he had something that was really worth an hour of the president's time, Sachs was ushered into the Oval Office.

"Alex," Roosevelt said, "what are you up to?"

Sachs felt that it would not be enough simply to hand the president the letter. He believed that a president saw so much paper that another letter, even from a figure as eminent as Albert Einstein, might not make a sufficient impression. So he decided to begin with a story that had first been related by Lord Acton, the noted British historian.

The story concerned a young American inventor who wrote a letter to Napoléon Bonaparte. Napoléon had been frustrated in his attempts to invade England because of the tricky tides and currents of the English Channel. The inventor told Napoléon that he could build a fleet of ships that needed no sails and could attack England in any weather. Napoléon was unimpressed at the idea of ships without sails. He dismissed the young man with the words, "Bah! Away with your visionists!"

The young American inventor, Sachs said, was Robert Fulton, inventor of the steamboat. Lord Acton had stated that the whole of 19th-century history might have been different if the emperor had paid attention to Fulton.

Sachs then told the president that he wanted him to listen very carefully because what he had to tell him was at least the equivalent of Robert Fulton's steamboat proposal. Roosevelt stopped him and summoned an aide and handed him a short note. The aide returned with a carefully wrapped bottle of rare and expensive Napoléon brandy and two glasses. The president filled the glasses and pushed one over to Sachs. He was ready to listen.

Sachs had thought long and hard about exactly how he was going to make this proposal to Roosevelt. Both Einstein and Szilard had prepared descriptions of the scientific basis of nuclear energy and what its implications might be. Sachs was no scientist, but neither was Roosevelt. He decided it would be best to prepare his own layperson's version of what the physicists had said.

He tried to emphasize some of the beneficial possibilities of the development of nuclear energy. But he also said that it could be used to produce "bombs of hitherto unenvisaged potency and scope."

He ended by saying that he had no doubt that at some time man would release and control almost unlimited power. "We cannot prevent him from doing so and can only hope that he will not use it exclusively in blowing up his next door neighbor."

The practical Roosevelt knew exactly what he was being asked to do. "Alex," he said, "what you are after is to see that the Nazis don't blow us up."

"Precisely," Sachs responded.

Roosevelt called in his chief aide. "This requires action," he said.[2]

And so a chain of events was set in motion that led to the explosion in the New Mexico desert and all that followed. But at first events did not move as swiftly as one might imagine. A small committee was set up called the

"Advisory Committee on Uranium," consisting of the head of the Bureau of Standards, who was a government scientist, and representatives of the army. The Hungarian scientists, Szilard, Wigner, and Teller, came to Washington to talk to them. The military representatives were not impressed by the theories of a group of "foreign" scientists. They weren't convinced that an atomic bomb could be produced at all, and even if it was they didn't think it would make much difference in a war.

But in the end they agreed to a relatively modest budget to fund further research into nuclear energy.

Chapter 2

"THE ITALIAN NAVIGATOR HAS JUST LANDED"

LEO SZILARD HAD ASKED FOR a comparatively modest $6,000 to construct a graphite-uranium system for producing a nuclear chain reaction. After some argument the uranium committee reluctantly agreed. But the money was painfully slow in arriving. The committee chairman, Dr. Lyman J. Briggs, director of the Bureau of Standards, was used to working on small projects with limited budgets. He also had an obsession with secrecy and a distrust of foreign scientists. He would not allow scientists like Szilard or the Nobel Prize–winning Italian physicist Enrico Fermi, who had jointly developed the graphite-uranium system, to take part in discussions of their own secrets. Briggs dissolved a special advisory committee of scientists after its first meeting. He blandly explained that if a chain reaction proved to be impossible, Congress might investigate. And the government would be embarrassed if the public knew that Washington had financed a project recommended by men who were not "Americans of long standing"—meaning most of the scientists involved. The refugee scientists felt humiliated, and some swore they would no longer work on the project in any capacity.

Szilard, who had finally obtained a paying job at Columbia University, loudly predicted all over the campus that Germany would now win the war. He was so outspoken that later investigations by Army Intelligence reported that he was "pro-German"—a mistaken conclusion. At one point there was even some discussion of having Szilard interned as an enemy alien. Wisely, the idea was dropped. But he was kept under close surveillance for many months.

The uranium committee was dragging its feet because the members didn't feel the urgency that animated Szilard and his colleagues. The homelands of the émigré scientists might have been overrun by the Nazis, but the United States wasn't at war. The possibility of war loomed, but the sentiment in America against getting involved in foreign wars was still very strong. And the members of the committee didn't really understand the science behind the possibility of an atomic bomb. There seemed no compelling reason to expend a lot of time and effort and money on a rush program to develop a weapon that might not be needed and probably wouldn't work anyhow. Those comfortable assumptions were about to be overtaken by events.

Hitler was sweeping across Europe. The British barely managed a humiliating evacuation at Dunkirk, and France simply surrendered. Britain itself was under ferocious air attack. The Germans turned eastward and invaded the Soviet Union, which appeared to be on the verge of crumbling. The headlines became more frightening every day, and America's eventual involvement in the war seemed more and more inevitable.

Refugee scientists in Britain like Otto Frisch and Rudolf Peierls were already engaged in nuclear research. Independently they arrived at the conclusion that an atomic bomb was not only feasible, but with the proper allocation of resources could be built in about two years.

For a brief time the British government toyed with the idea of an independent A-bomb research project, perhaps in Canada, where it would be safe from German bombs. But it just wasn't possible. Britain's resources were stretched to the limit and committed to the development of things that would have a more immediate military application, like radar. If an atomic bomb was to be developed outside of Germany it would have to be in America. British scientists began to vigorously lobby their American colleagues as to the importance of A-bomb research. And their voices were being heard as more and more American scientists threw their prestige behind an accelerated program of nuclear weapons research.

There were ominous rumors about German progress in this area. When the Germans conquered Belgium they also took control over what was then the Belgian Congo in Africa, where some of the richest uranium deposits in the world were located. When they overran Norway they took over the world's only plant manufacturing "heavy water" (oxygen and an isotope of hydrogen). The Germans were convinced that heavy water was essential for the operation of a nuclear reactor. But the substance was extremely scarce and difficult to manufacture.

Despite the departure of many—mainly Jewish—physicists from Germany or areas under German control, there was still an impressive list of scientists available to work on a German bomb. Heading the list was Werner

Heisenberg—by any measure one of the greatest scientists of the 20th century.

The possibility that Hitler might soon have access to the most powerful weapon the world had ever known seemed frighteningly real.

Then came December 7, 1941. The Japanese allies of Germany bombed Pearl Harbor and instantly war became a reality for the United States. There was no longer any question that the development of an atomic bomb was to become a top military priority.

Even before the U.S. entry into the war the pace of U.S. atomic bomb research had picked up. In November 1940 the U.S. government appropriated $40,000 to construct a system suggested by Szilard but designed by Enrico Fermi, to develop a self-sustaining chain reaction—the key to unleashing the power of the atom. The system was based not on heavy water but on the use of uranium and graphite, the latter a form of carbon and the black greasy material that is found in "lead" pencils.

Work began at Columbia University but was soon shifted to the University of Chicago. The first choice for a site to construct the atomic pile for the experiment was in a part of the Cook County Forest Preserve, some 20 miles (32 kilometers) southwest of Chicago, known as the Argonne forest. But a strike delayed construction, and an alternative site had to be chosen quickly. It was the squash court beneath the University of Chicago's Stagg Field. The athletic field was largely unused since the university abandoned its intercollegiate sports program. The scientists had already used the area for other experiments.

This was a fateful decision. The experiment would be conducted right in the middle of a major metropolitan area, and nobody really knew how it would come out. Fermi was convinced that the reaction could be controlled and posed no danger except possibly to those who were actually carrying out the experiment—and he was going to be one of them—so he was putting his own life on the line. Still, says Richard Rhodes (author of *The Making of the Atomic Bomb*) what the scientists were risking was "a small Chernobyl in the midst of a crowded city."[1] By now, however, the project had become so urgent that the Stagg Field site was approved immediately. The president of the University of Chicago was never informed about what was going on, because he certainly would have tried to stop the project.[2]

The key experiment was performed on December 2, 1942, a bitterly cold day. Though Fermi and others had calculated that the possibility of a disaster was extremely low, it is not the sort of experiment that would have been performed in peacetime. But it wasn't peacetime anymore.

Rhodes sets the scene:

"Outside was raw wind. On the second day of gasoline rationing Chicagoans jammed streetcars and elevated trains, leaving almost half their usual traffic of automobiles at home. The State Department had announced that morning that two million Jews had perished in Europe and five million more were in danger. The Germans were preparing counterattacks in North Africa; American marines and Japanese soldiers struggled in the hell of Guadalcanal."[3]

The center of the experiment was the atomic "pile"—a nearly 500-ton pile of graphite bricks, stacked in 57 layers, into which cubes of uranium or uranium oxide were embedded. Two shifts of workers had labored 16 days to build the 20-foot (6-meter)-high structure. There were no blue-

This is the only photo of the first nuclear reactor. It was taken as the nineteenth layer of graphite was being put into place.

prints or plans, just Fermi's calculations, and on December 2 he decided that the pile was big enough.

Long control rods, plated with the element cadmium, were set up so they could be inserted into holes in the graphite bricks and withdrawn when required. The graphite would slow down the neutrons emitted by the uranium, and the cadmium would absorb them. As the control rods were withdrawn, however, fewer of the neutrons from the uranium would be absorbed, resulting in greater fission—more atoms split. At some point as the rods were withdrawn, fission would produce neutrons faster than the cadmium would absorb them. The result would be a self-sustaining chain reaction. This is the action basic to the atomic bomb or any other release of nuclear power.

About 40 senior scientists crammed into the balcony overlooking the squash court. There was no heat on the court, so everyone was wearing coats and hats, scarves and gloves. The air was filled with graphite dust, and a thick layer of dust coating the floor made it slippery.

Three young men perched on a platform above the pile. They were dubbed the "suicide squad," ready to douse the pile with a cadmium salt solution if the experiment began to go out of control.

There was only one man on the floor, George Weil, a young physicist who would slowly pull the last control rod out of the pile. A safety rod controlled by a solenoid-activated catch was designed to automatically fall into place and stop the chain reaction if neutron activity exceeded a preset level. Another rod hung suspended from the balcony. One of the project leaders, armed with an ax, was ready to chop the rope so the rod would drop into the pile and presumably stop the reaction if things went disastrously wrong.

Fermi acted as overseer and impresario. "George will pull out his rod a little at a time," he said. "We shall take measurements and verify that the pile will keep on acting as we have calculated."

The experiment began exactly at 10:37 that morning when Fermi instructed Weil to begin removing the last cadmium rod. The neutron counters began clicking. Fermi had his 6-inch (15-centimeter) slide rule, the pocket calculator of its day, and was carefully calculating the rate of increase. It met his expectations so he told Weil to move the rod out another 6 inches (15 centimeters). Once again the clicking increased. Again Fermi checked his calculations and seemed pleased.

The process continued for about an hour. Suddenly there was a loud crash. The safety rod had been automatically released. The release was unexpected, but Fermi knew the pile was still subcritical. Fermi, a man of regular habits said, "I'm hungry. Let's go to lunch."

At two in the afternoon the safety rod was reset and the experiment continued. At 3:25 Fermi ordered Weil to pull the control rod out another 12 inches (30 centimeters). "This is going to do it," he said. "Now it will become self-sustaining. The trace [on the recorder] will climb and continue to climb, it will not level off."

An eyewitness recalled: "Again and again, the scale of the recorder had to be changed to accommodate the neutron intensity, which was increasing more and more rapidly. Suddenly Fermi raised his hand, 'The pile has gone critical,' he announced. No one present had any doubt that he was right.[4]

Fermi grinned. Then everyone began to wonder why he didn't shut the pile down. But he was completely calm. He waited one minute, then another, and then when the anxiety seemed too much to bear, he ordered the control rod be reinserted.

It was 3:53 P.M. This was the first controlled release of the energy from the atomic nucleus. Eugene Wigner recalled that while everyone had expected the success of the experiment, ". . . its accomplishment had a deep impact on us. For some time we had known that we were about to unlock a giant; still we could not escape an eerie feeling when we had actually done it. . . ."

Many consider that moment in the freezing squash court at the University of Chicago the key step in the development of the atomic bomb. The basic principle of a self-sustaining chain reaction had been demonstrated beyond any doubt. After that it was all "engineering."

To celebrate their success, Wigner produced a bottle of Italian Chianti. Because of the war the importation of Italian wine had been banned for months. Wigner had to search liquor stores all over Chicago for a bottle. He produced it from a paper bag and everyone drank a small amount from a paper cup. Then Fermi signed the straw wrapping on the bottle and passed it around so others could sign.

One of the scientists called a colleague in Washington and reported in an improvised code, "You'll be interested to know that the Italian navigator has just landed in the new world. . . ."

"Were the natives friendly?" was the response.

"Everyone landed safe and happy."[5]

Not everyone was happy. Leo Szilard, who had been instrumental in bringing this moment about, had watched the proceedings from the balcony. He waited until everybody but Fermi had left. "I shook hands with Fermi and I said I thought this day would go down as a black day in the history of mankind."

Chapter 3

THE ODD COUPLE

IN THE MONTHS THAT FOLLOWED Pearl Harbor the Manhattan Project—the name given to the atomic-bomb program because its original offices had been in Manhattan—grew rapidly. The army had been involved since June 1942 and by the fall the secretary of war realized that someone was going to have to be put in overall charge. The man who was chosen was Leslie Richard Groves, a 46-year-old colonel in the Army Corps of Engineers.

It was not an assignment that Colonel Groves had wanted, and when it was handed to him on September 17, 1942, he said that he was "probably the angriest officer in the United States Army."

Colonel Groves had been in charge of all military construction and was completing his biggest and most visible job—the Pentagon, the world's largest office building at the time. It was an important job, but now there was a war on and nobody remembered battles fought on construction lots. Groves wanted an overseas combat assignment.

Instead, his commanding officer told him that the secretary of war had selected him for a very important assignment in Washington. Groves said he didn't want to stay in Washington. But he was told, "If you do the job right it will win the war."

It should have been a historic moment, but all Groves could say was "Oh, that thing."

As deputy chief of construction for the entire U.S. Army, Groves had heard something about the bomb project, but he doubted that it would be decisive in winning the war. While building the Pentagon he spent more in a week than the entire budget for the Manhattan Project. The job he was now being given seemed like a real comedown. His feeling of disappointment was eased somewhat when he was told that he would immediately be promoted to brigadier general. As one of the oldest colonels in the army, Groves had often wondered if he would ever make general.

General Groves was a big man—almost 6 feet (2 meters) tall, and he probably weighed over 250 pounds (113 kilograms). Groves's father had been an army chaplain on the western frontier. As a boy he had lived on army bases, and while growing up his greatest ambition was to go to West Point. He did and graduated fourth in his class. When he was given the Manhattan Project he was married and had a 13-year-old daughter and a son at West Point.

General Leslie Groves was army through and through. One of his subordinates described him as "the biggest sonavabitch I've ever met in my life, but also one of the most capable individuals. He had an ego second to none, he had tireless energy—he was a big man, a heavy man but he never seemed to tire. He had absolute confidence in his

*Major General
Leslie Groves*

decisions and he was absolutely ruthless in how he approached a problem to get it done. But that was the beauty of working for him—you never had to worry about the decisions being made or what it meant. In fact I've often thought that if I were to have to do my part over again, I would select Groves as boss. I hated his guts and so did everybody else but we had our form of understanding."[1]

Within days after he was appointed, General Groves had made quick decisions on problems that had lingered for months.

Groves had a well-deserved reputation for bullying and humiliating people. Once in front of a meeting of scientists he took off his jacket and barked at his deputy, "Here, have this dry-cleaned." He was narrow-minded and deeply distrustful of anyone who was not just exactly like he was.

He had no qualms at all about spying on people and reading their private mail.

One government scientist who had met Groves briefly wrote: "I doubt whether he has sufficient tact for such a job. I fear we are in the soup."

The "soup" was that the bullying tactics that worked with his subordinates in the army, Washington bureaucrats, and representatives of companies that were needed to supply the materials for the Manhattan Project—everything from uranium to lumber—were not going to work on a group of the best scientists in the world. Such individuals were generally free spirits who ignored authority when they did not actually detest it. Groves didn't like them very much and had a tendency to treat Nobel Prize winners like army privates. Yet it was the scientists who were going to be the key to the success or failure of the Manhattan Project.

Another problem was that Groves, while a competent engineer, was no scientist. He didn't really understand the science behind building an atomic bomb, and he didn't pretend to. Someone else was going to be needed—a respected scientist who would really supervise the scientific side of the project and whose authority would be nearly as great as that of Groves himself.

General Groves had several people in mind. Top of his list was Ernest Lawrence of California, a practical, hardworking man whom Groves could relate to. But Lawrence was already doing essential work for the war effort. Other candidates were rejected for a variety of reasons—too young, uninterested, too theoretical, etc. Finally Groves focused on someone who on the surface seemed the most improbable candidate of all, 38-year-old J. Robert Oppenheimer. Sometimes called Robert or "Oppie" by his friends (never Bob), Oppenheimer was one of many scientists who was already at work on the bomb, though he and Groves had barely met.

The contrasts between Groves and Oppenheimer were absolutely stark—starting with appearance. While Groves was tall and heavy, Oppenheimer was taller and thin as a string bean. He weighed a mere 135 pounds (61 kilograms)—and was down to a dangerous 113 pounds (51 kilograms) by the time his work was finished. Groves was a nonsmoker, nearly a nondrinker, and disapproved of both. Oppenheimer was a five-pack-a-day man who made a fetish of mixing martinis.

Their backgrounds could hardly have been more different. Groves, the army "brat," was the straitlaced religious son of a Presbyterian chaplain. Oppenheimer came from a wealthy but nonobservant Jewish businessman's family. He was educated at New York City's Ethical Culture School and some of the best universities in America and Europe. Along with science he had an insatiable interest in a huge variety of other subjects—Hindu philosophy for one and had even mastered Sanskrit, the ancient sacred language of the Hindus, so he could read the Hindu classics in their original language. While Groves was no bigot, he had a gut level distrust of Jews, particularly nonreligious Jews like Oppenheimer. He didn't think they had strong moral values.

The two shared some characteristics, though not the sort that would seem to lead to a harmonious partnership. Like Groves, Oppenheimer was extremely egotistical and sure of himself. He did not bully or humiliate people, but he could be caustic and cutting and he had offended many. He admitted that he often behaved in a "beastly" manner.

Dr. J. Robert Oppenheimer

Oppenheimer was an absolutely brilliant man, everyone acknowledged that, but he had not won a Nobel Prize, though some of those who would be working under him had. It was often said that Oppie lacked the discipline to apply himself to a single problem long enough to do Nobel Prize quality work. He was a theoretical physicist rather than a practical experimentalist like Lawrence. Indeed Oppenheimer had a reputation for being very clumsy in performing experiments. The bomb project seemed to require a more practical, hands-on scientist. And worst of all, the position seemed to require strong administrative experience, and Oppenheimer had never administered anything. He sort of floated from one university to another doing work that he found interesting.

Then there was politics. General Groves hated the Nazis, but he didn't think much more of Communists. As a young man Robert Oppenheimer showed almost no interest in politics. He rarely even read the newspapers. When the stock market crashed in 1929, it was days before Oppenheimer even heard about it, and then he didn't care very much. But the ravages of the Great Depression and the rise of Hitler changed him. He became an ardent left-winger. He contributed to a wide spectrum of left-wing causes, subscribed to many left-wing publications, spoke at meetings, even stuffed envelopes for the local teachers' union. He was never a Communist, but his brother, sister-in-law, former fiancée, and wife all had been. So were many of his closest friends.

One FBI agent even advised that Oppenheimer be considered for custodial detention "in the event of a National Emergency." Groves read the FBI's dossier on Oppenheimer and was not concerned. He thought that Oppenheimer was the best man available for the job, so instead of being put in jail for the duration of the war, Robert Oppenheimer was being offered what was probably the most sensitive security position in the country. And he quickly jumped at the opportunity.

When General Groves appointed Oppenheimer the project's scientific director practically everyone was astonished. Physicist Isidore I. Rabi later commented that Oppenheimer's appointment "was a real stroke of genius on the part of General Groves, who was not generally considered to be a genius. . . ."[2]

It was true that the most obvious candidates were unavailable, and the success of the project itself was very much in doubt, but there were plenty of more obvious choices.

Leslie Groves had seen something in Robert Oppenheimer that overcame all the possible objections—he saw that Oppenheimer desperately wanted the job, that he had confidence in the project, and that he would do absolutely anything to make sure that it succeeded.

It also appears that Groves genuinely liked Oppenheimer. "He's a genius," he told an interviewer after the war. "A real genius. While Lawrence is very bright he's not a genius, just a good hard worker. Why, Oppenheimer knows about everything. He can talk to you about anything you bring up. Well not exactly. I guess there are a few things he doesn't know about. He doesn't know anything about sports."[3]

That was a shortcoming that the general, who was an avid sports fan and often used baseball metaphors to express himself, must have keenly felt.

To those who questioned Oppenheimer's leadership qualities and had reservations about his appointment, Groves said, "Find me another Ernest Lawrence, and we'll appoint him. But where do you find such a man? With Oppenheimer we at least have a first-rate theoretician and an extremely brilliant mind. As for the administration, I will see that it works!"[4]

Unlike some of the Manhattan Project scientists, Oppenheimer always treated General Groves with respect. Even in private he is not known to have called him anything worse than "his Nibs." He explained the scientific principles to Groves more clearly than anyone else had, and if the general still did not understand, he explained them again. Oppenheimer was well aware that he could not afford to be beastly to General Groves if the project were to succeed.

Oppenheimer quickly presented one idea that Groves liked very much. In 1942 the Manhattan Project's scientists were scattered all over the map, working out of different laboratories—some were at Chicago, some at Columbia, others at different universities throughout the country. Morale was terrible and communication difficult. Security, an obsession with Groves, was not merely a headache, it was a nightmare. Oppenheimer proposed a unified separate laboratory to focus exclusively on the weapon itself: working out the unknowns of its explosion, designing it, building it, testing, and using it on the enemy in time to end the war. The laboratory could be built in some isolated place, which would help preserve security, but still allow the scientists to talk freely with one another.

Groves was delighted because he had been thinking along the same lines. Privately Groves regarded most scientists as "crackpots" and "prima donnas" who talked too much anyway. But at least if they were all in one place, surrounded by barbed wire, they could be watched.

When Groves suggested that the scientists could be drafted, wear uniforms, and become subject to military discipline, Oppenheimer agreed. He even reported to San Francisco's Presidio for his army physical. Oppenheimer was declared fit to be a lieutenant colonel even though he was nearly 30 pounds (14 kilograms) underweight, had a chronic cough, and a history of tuberculosis. Other scientists were not nearly as willing to start wearing uniforms and saluting. Some threatened to quit the project, and the idea of drafting the scientists into the army was quietly shelved.

Once when Groves was asked how he was able to get along so well with Oppenheimer, who was in so many ways his complete opposite, Groves replied, "Maybe because Dr. Oppenheimer agrees with me."

After Oppenheimer was officially given the job of the laboratory's director, he embarked on a campaign "of absolutely unscrupulous recruiting of anyone we can lay hands on." Oppenheimer couldn't bully and order like Groves. He used his formidable charm to cajole, flatter, and dazzle some of the best scientific talent in the country to join in the search for the atomic bomb.

The next big task was to find a location for his bomb-making laboratory, tentatively called "Site Y." Oppenheimer may have had a location in mind already—but he didn't say anything at first. Appearing to order General Groves around would not have been a tactful move.

Chapter 4

LOS ALAMOS

SITE Y HAD TO HAVE good transportation, an adequate supply of water, a local labor force, and a moderate climate for year-round construction and outdoor experiments. Other criteria for the site were that it had to be at least 200 miles (322 kilometers) from any international boundary but west of the Mississippi. Some existing facilities should already be at the site, and it should be located in a natural bowl, with the hills that shaped the bowl nearby so that fences might be built on the hills and guarded. General Groves later said that the site had to be isolated so as to protect nearby communities from "any unforeseen results from our activities." That was not, of course, the whole story. The high barbed-wire fence that ultimately surrounded the Manhattan Project laboratory was not built to confine explosions. It was meant to keep casual visitors out and keep the scientists in.

A number of sites in the Southwest were explored. On November 16, Oppenheimer, Groves, and representatives from the Army Corps of Engineers were inspecting a site at Jemez Springs, New Mexico, a deep canyon about 40 miles (64 kilometers) northwest of Santa Fe. Oppenheimer found the canyon rather depressing and expressed his reservations. Groves, who had a sore arm and was in a bad mood, liked it even less. "This will never do," he said. His main objection was that the canyon prevented expansion. An experienced engineer, Groves knew that no matter what size limit is set, projects almost inevitably grow larger than anyone predicted.

At this point Oppenheimer said innocently, "Well, we can go back to Albuquerque by way of the Los Alamos Ranch School. You might be interested in that."

This was an area that Oppenheimer knew well. He owned a small ranch about 50 miles (80 kilometers) from Los Alamos, and he had ridden there many times. The name *Los Alamos* means "the cottonwoods." Later Oppenheimer admitted that Los Alamos had always been his secret choice for the project's location.

When he was a boy Oppenheimer had suffered from trench dysentery and colitis. He was sent to the Southwest because it was believed that the dry desert climate would be good for his health. It was, and Oppenheimer fell in love with the area, returning to it as often as he could and eventually buying a ranch there. "My two great loves are physics and desert country," he once said. "It's a pity they can't be combined." They were just about to be.

The large military sedan bearing Oppenheimer, Groves, and two other officers pulled up at Fuller Lodge, the large, rustic main house of the Los Alamos Ranch School, in the late afternoon. In one very obvious way the spot failed to fulfill Groves's criteria. It was located on a mesa—high ground, not in a canyon as he had wanted. But still it could easily be fenced—Groves liked it at once.

The school had been built to cater to the sons of affluent families in the East. The boys slept in unheated cabins, took cold showers, and wore shorts, even in the winter. When the site selection party arrived the boys were playing soccer in shorts, and it was snowing! The aim was to toughen up soft and sickly city boys.

If Los Alamos was chosen water would be a problem if a large number of people were to be housed there. The main road—it led to Santa Fe about 30 miles (48 kilometers) southeast—was horrible, even by local standards. But Groves quickly decided both problems would be fixable. The existing log cabins would serve as a nucleus for the housing to come. The setting was magnificent, giving breathtaking views of the Jemez Mountains and the Sangre de Cristo mountain range. This would certainly be a lure for the "prima donna" scientists, as Groves called them. It was an awesome setting for developing the most awesome weapon the human race had ever seen.

Groves moved quickly. He called Washington that evening to begin buying the land. By 1942 the Los Alamos Ranch School had fallen on hard financial times because of the war. The school was more than happy to sell out and the deal was completed within a week. The land, the buildings, and other possessions of the school, including 1,600 books and 60 horses, went for $440,000. In a month the first of 3,000 construction men moved in and began work.

Robert Oppenheimer began shuttling around the country recruiting the best scientists by telling them that they would be working on a New Mexico mountaintop in a setting of epic beauty and what they were doing would end

The main building of the Los Alamos Ranch School

the war. It was a good pitch, and he signed up some of the best—like Edward Teller and Hans Bethe. Enrico Fermi agreed to shuttle from Chicago as often as his commitments would allow—and he eventually wound up settling at Los Alamos. Isidore Rabi, who was busy perfecting radar at the Massachusetts Institute of Technology, made himself available as Oppie's senior consultant.

Oppie's sales pitch was so enthusiastic that one of the scientists he recruited recalled, "I thought he had a screw loose somewhere."

Not everyone was taken with the vision of the lab on the mountaintop. The irascible Leo Szilard was a man of the cities. He said that "nobody could think straight at a place like that. Everybody will go crazy."[1]

By March 1943, Oppenheimer was at Los Alamos, and he seemed to be everywhere, rushing from place to place in his curious loping run. His "uniform"—a crumpled suit and porkpie hat—were to become a familiar sight.

Los Alamos or "the Hill" as everybody began to call it, officially opened for business on April 15. About 50 scientists were already there. Groves greeted each of them with a handshake and a lecture about how if they failed he was going to have to go to Congress and justify wasting all that money. That greeting did not go down well.

Then the scientists began doing exactly what Groves had feared they would do—talking freely to one another. Groves had placed great faith in what he called "compartmentalization"—each scientist or team of scientists was to work within a narrow area and not discuss their work with others. Only a few top people would have a whole picture of what was going on. The less information an individual had the less he could potentially betray. But for the scientists, openness and a free exchange of ideas were essential, even in a secret wartime project. The general began to feel as though he were sponsoring a free-for-all gabfest for gossips and spies.

Oppenheimer insisted on one modest code word or euphemism—what they were building was never called "the bomb," it was always "the gadget."

While the critical experiment of establishing the possibility of a chain reaction may have been performed by Fermi in Chicago, the technical problems of turning a theory into a weapon were enormous.

One of the weekly meetings at Los Alamos for exchanging ideas among scientists at work on various parts of the Manhattan Project. Shown here are, third from the left in the front row, Enrico Fermi and, in the second row, J. Robert Oppenheimer and Richard Feynman, who would win the 1965 Nobel Prize for physics for his work in quantum electrodynamics.

There were really two types of atomic weapons being prepared at Los Alamos. The first utilized the rare isotope uranium 235. It would be detonated by using a modified artillery gun inside a bomb casing to fire a lump of uranium onto a spherical uranium target at 2,000 feet (610 meters) per second. The impact of one subcritical mass onto the other would produce a nuclear explosion. The problem was that uranium 235 was so rare that there probably would only be enough of it to produce a single bomb over the next two years.

Theoretically an atomic bomb could also be produced using the artificial element plutonium. No one at Los Alamos had ever actually seen a sample of plutonium, but they were reasonably sure that enough of it would become available to make more than one bomb. By July, however, the scientists had concluded that this relatively simple "gun assembly" method probably would not work for the plutonium bomb. The two subcritical masses of plutonium could not be brought together fast enough to prevent a premature detonation.

The solution to this dilemma was suggested by one of Oppenheimer's former students, physicist Seth Neddermeyer. He proposed that the plutonium should be surrounded by a layer of high explosives. When the explosives were detonated, they focused the blast wave so as to compress the plutonium instantly into a supercritical mass. It was the theory of "implosion." This was a much more complicated procedure, and most of the scientists who first heard the theory did not think it could be made to work. Oppenheimer himself was far from enthusiastic; it seemed too complicated to be brought off in time to affect the war, but he grudgingly conceded that "this has to be looked into." It was ultimately the theory of implosion that led to the single most significant breakthrough accomplished at Los Alamos. While many of the atomic "secrets" were not secrets at all—implosion was. In fact, the very word *implosion* remained a classified secret until six years after the war was over.

Neddermeyer's implosion theory got a tremendous boost when the mathematician John von Neumann calculated that implosion was indeed feasible and that it would require less of the precious fissionable material than the gun method. Von Neumann, who was the founder of the game theory and a pioneer in computers, was a man whom even geniuses did not hesitate to call a genius. When he delivered an opinion at Los Alamos, everyone listened.

Edward Teller had yet another idea—bypass the atomic bomb entirely and produce a weapon that he called "the super." He speculated that the incredible amount of heat that would build up within an exploding atomic, or fission, bomb could be used to ignite hydrogen. This would be a fusion bomb—what we now call a hydrogen bomb. Teller believed that such a weapon would be cheaper and infinitely more powerful than a fission bomb. While Teller continued to agitate for his fusion bomb, it did not become a major issue until the war was over and the Manhattan Project ended.

One day during a meeting of the top scientists, Teller strode to the blackboard and scrawled a series of calculations showing how effectively an atomic bomb explosion would detonate a fusion reaction. Unfortunately, he said that it might also set the oceans and atmosphere on fire and destroy all life on Earth. Oppenheimer immediately called an end to the meeting. He took a train to Michigan to consult with Arthur Holly Compton, the Nobel Prize–winning physicist and his superior in the bomb project. Compton was horrified.

"This would be the ultimate catastrophe," he cried. "Better to accept the slavery of the Nazis than run a chance of drawing a final curtain on mankind!"[2]

Everybody breathed a huge sigh of relief when it was discovered that Teller had made some errors in his calculations. There was apparently only one chance in 3 million of the atomic bomb igniting the atmosphere. Still, the fear that the bomb would abruptly make the planet uninhabitable lingered in the back of the minds of those who knew what the Manhattan Project was really trying to accomplish.

Before the laboratory at Los Alamos opened, Oppenheimer drew up an organizational chart and figured he would need about 30 men to build the bomb. His assistants were shocked, so he upped the estimate to about 100. Oppenheimer's 100-man staff ultimately grew to more than 4,000 civilians and 2,000 military working in almost 250 buildings and living in more than 500 apartment houses, dormitories, and trailers.

The nearest town to Los Alamos was Santa Fe. The people of Santa Fe knew that something was going on at "the Hill," but no one was really sure what. Many rumors circulated, most wide of the mark. It was supposed to be a poison gas factory, a concentration camp, even some sort of a hospital, because there were so many "doctors" there. Oppenheimer had people deliberately spread the false rumor that they were working on an "electric rocket" and that story was widely believed. Mail to Los Alamos came addressed simply to "Box 1663, Sandoval County, Rural."

The housing accommodations were anything but luxurious. The scientists, technicians, and their families moved into prefabricated army houses and thin-walled apartments with heaters that didn't work and wood-burning stoves that didn't light. Only the most senior men and their families were allowed to settle in the former homes of the Ranch School faculty, and these had bathtubs. The new housing only had showers. "Bathtub Row" was the supreme status neighborhood at Los Alamos.

Aside from work there wasn't really a great deal to do at Los Alamos. Movies sent there were well attended. There were amateur theatricals. In a production of *Arsenic and Old Lace*, Oppenheimer played a corpse. There were also a lot of babies born among the Los Alamos families. The economy-minded Groves grumbled that couples were simply "taking advantage" of the free medical care.

Security was the most oppressive feature. Husbands were not even supposed to tell their wives what they were doing. Phone calls were monitored. Mail was opened and read. Army intelligence agents were everywhere, openly listening in on people's private conversations. The barbed wire bothered many, particularly the European-born scientists. There actually were spies at Los Alamos—but they were never detected by the security.

Despite a great deal of grumbling, only one scientist quit the project because he resented the military intrusion in his life, and he was an unlikely defector. Edward U. Condon was picked to be Oppenheimer's deputy director. The crew-cut, bull-necked Condon was the son of a western mining engineer and had been born in New Mexico, not far from Los Alamos. But after a few weeks he got into a dispute with Groves, and when he felt that Oppenheimer was not backing him up he resigned in a fury.

Groves was later to say that one of his biggest tasks at Los Alamos was to keep the prima donna scientists happy. This was a task at which he did not succeed. The scientists not only grumbled, they struck back in a variety of ways—and since there was a very high percentage of geniuses among them, some of the ways could be—well—ingenious. Twenty-five-year-old Richard Feynman got a reputation as

The Winchester Company, one of the United States's leading arms manufacturers, posted warnings like this all over their plant, as did many other companies that were involved in the production of wartime materials.

the project's comedian. He figured out the combination to many of the office safes, which contained sensitive material. He would open them and leave little notes saying: "Guess Who."[3]

One scientist was admonished for leaving highly classified technical documents on his desk overnight—in defiance of all security regulations. He replied airily that some of the calculations in the documents were wrong and any spy was welcome to them.

The scientists were impossible to discipline. They worked whatever hours they chose, wandered in and out of the mess hall at any hour. Edward Teller liked to play the piano—and he did frequently until three in the morning—much to the consternation of his neighbors who could hear every note through the thin walls.

For a period Los Alamos contained the greatest collection of scientific geniuses in one place that the world had ever seen. They were working on a project that they hoped would win the greatest war the world had ever seen, but they feared it would change the course of history in unforeseeable and possibly disastrous ways. And they were working under a tight deadline. There had never been anything like Los Alamos before, or since—yet somehow it all came together.

Chapter 5

THE GERMAN BOMB PROJECT

AT LOS ALAMOS, and among all of those elsewhere in the United States and Great Britain who knew about the possibility of an atomic bomb, the desire to find out what the Germans were doing—and stop them—became an obsession.

Germany certainly possessed the scientific and technical knowledge and the industrial capacity to produce an atomic bomb. To many it appeared as if the Germans were the real leaders in the field of atomic research. But very early on the German attempts to produce atomic weapons took a serious wrong turn.

One of the things that scientists had to discover to successfully carry out experiments in this field was a proper "moderator" in which to encase uranium and thus slow down the neutrons in the fission process. It was crucial that the moderator itself absorb few neutrons. The two chief candidates were carbon and the curiously named heavy water (a substance that contains oxygen and a rare form of hydrogen called deuterium).

Working at Columbia University, Enrico Fermi and his associate, Herbert L. Anderson, had discovered that pure carbon would almost certainly be a perfect moderator. Under normal circumstances they would have published an article on their work with one of the leading scientific journals, making their results available to the world scientific community. In fact, Fermi and Anderson had actually written such a paper, but they agreed not to publish it. By 1939 there was a general moratorium on publishing any scientific research that might help the Germans build an atomic bomb. Fermi then went on to try graphite, a form of carbon, in his crucial experiment at the University of Chicago, which produced in December 1942 the first self-sustaining chain reaction.

In the meantime the German scientist Walter Bothe was experimenting with an impure batch of carbon. He concluded, incorrectly, that carbon would not be an adequate neutron moderator. If he had been able to read Fermi and Anderson's unpublished article Bothe would have known where he had gone wrong.

But the Germans did not get this information and were left to rely on the rare and difficult to produce heavy water. After their conquest of Norway, the Germans came into possession of one of the only facilities in the world capable of producing heavy water in any quantity. It was located at Vemork in southern Norway. The plant became an important target for the Allies in the secret war against the German bomb.

Shortly after his appointment as head of the Manhattan Project, General Groves requested action against the plant. The British had already been planning to send two glider loads of demolition experts, 34 trained volunteers, to destroy the plant. On November 19, 1942, an advance party of four Norwegian commandos parachuted into the area. But the next night brought disaster. The gliders crossed the North Sea from Scotland; both crashed in Norway, and the 14 men who survived the disaster were captured by the Germans and executed the same day.

Destruction of the heavy-water plant was considered so important that the British ordered another raid. This time six specially trained Norwegians parachuted onto a frozen lake 30 miles (48 kilometers) northwest of the plant on February 16, 1943. They had skis, supplies, a shortwave radio, plastic explosives, and cyanide capsules, in case they were captured. After enduring a fierce storm, they were able to rendezvous with the four Norwegians of the original advance party. The four had been hiding, were near starvation, and desperate to get the supplies.

One of the party skied over to the plant to gather the latest information. He found that since the failed glider attack plant security had been improved, but still only 15 German soldiers were on duty.

The commandos set out to attack the plant on the evening of February 27. It was a massive seven-story structure. Wrote one of the commandos: "We understood how the Germans could allow themselves to keep so small a guard there. The colossus lay like a medieval castle built in the most inaccessible place, protected by precipices and rivers."[1]

The commandos had a significant advantage. One of the men who had helped build part of the plant had escaped to Britain and was working for British intelligence. He had identified a cable intake that bypassed most of the defenses and led directly to the heavy-water facility. Two men were able to crawl through and leave a bomb in place without being detected.

After a short wait there was what sounded like a small explosion. The German guards barely noticed. They checked the doors, found them still locked and returned to their quarters. The Norwegians made a quick escape before the sirens began going off. The operation was a complete success. No one was injured on either side. The plant could certainly be repaired, but the German physicists were going to have a lot less heavy water for now.

At first the British estimated that the plant would be out of operation for at least a year, probably two. But reports filtered back that the Germans had mounted a major repair effort. Increased German security at the plant made another commando raid impossible.

Groves began pushing for stronger action. Just before dawn on November 16, 1943, 200 U.S. B-17 Flying Fortresses from the 3rd Bomber Division took off from British airfields. The planes dropped some 400 tons of bombs on the plant and surrounding area. The bombs were dropped from a high altitude and were not very accurate. In fact, only 12 bombs actually hit the plant itself. But limited as the damage was, it succeeded in shutting down the plant and convinced the Germans there was no point in trying to put it back into operation because there was no way to defend it completely.

Over the next few months the Norwegian heavy-water equipment was dismantled and sent to Germany. In February 1944 the last of the heavy water, about 1,323 pounds (600 kilograms) in 40 drums of water was shipped from Rjukan. But the Allies got wind of the shipment and were determined to stop it.

The Norwegian underground was contacted. It was determined that the drums of heavy water would be shipped by train to the head of Lake Tinnsjo. At that point they would be loaded on a ferry bound for Germany. Blowing up the train would be difficult, sinking the ferry was a better plan. Sinking the ferry, however, would undoubtedly cause a number of deaths, among both the Norwegian passengers and the German guards. Killing the guards would almost certainly call down heavy reprisals against the Norwegian population. The Norwegians questioned whether the sabotage operation would be worthwhile.

The reply from London came immediately via clandestine shortwave radio.

"Matter has been considered. It is thought very important that heavy water shall be destroyed. Hope it can be done without too disastrous results. Send our best wishes for success in the work. Greetings."[2]

Members of the Norwegian underground snuck aboard the ferry with the help of a sympathetic watchman. Below deck they placed an explosive charge with two alarm-clock timers. Ten minutes later they were off the boat and on their way to neutral Sweden. Forty-five minutes into its voyage the bomb exploded. Twenty-six passengers and crew members drowned, and the drums of heavy water rolled overboard and sank to the bottom of the lake.

In an interview given after the war a German explosives expert said: "When one considers that right up to the end of the war, in 1945, there was virtually no increase in our heavy-water stocks in Germany . . . it will be seen that it was the elimination of German heavy-water production in Norway that was the main factor in our failure to achieve a self-sustaining atomic reactor before the war ended."[3]

The race for the bomb may have ended for Germany on that mountain lake in Norway in February 1944.

But the Americans and the British didn't want to take any chances. Groves continued to press for bombing raids on the laboratories where it was believed that German scientists were at work on an atomic bomb. And Groves's own office in Washington began to organize an aggressive campaign to identify, locate, and lay hands on the men building Hitler's bomb.

Top of the list was the great German physicist Werner Heisenberg. Before the war Heisenberg had been a highly respected member of the international community of scientists, but when the war came he committed himself fully to the German cause. Though he was not, as far as can be determined, a Nazi, he was a German nationalist and had come to the conclusion that Hitler was better than Stalin, and if it came to a choice a Nazi conquest of Europe was preferable.

In September 1941, Heisenberg met with his old teacher and friend, the almost legendary Danish physicist Niels Bohr, in Denmark. Recollections differ as to exactly what was said at this meeting, but Heisenberg left the distinct impression that the Germans were hard at work on the bomb and that Bohr should try to persuade the physicists in America that they should all join in an effort to convince all of the world's scientists not to do any atomic-bomb research for any country.

During the conversation Heisenberg handed Bohr a drawing of an experimental heavy-water reactor he was working on. Why he did this is not clear even today. If he did it clandestinely, then he risked his life, for he was almost certainly being watched by Nazi agents. If he did it cynically and with Nazi approval, he may have been trying to mislead Bohr about the quality and direction of German atomic research.

At this point Bohr knew little about the research that was going on in Britain and America, and was profoundly shocked that the Germans were so heavily involved in an atomic-bomb project. He suspected that Heisenberg was acting as an agent for the Nazi government, and the long-time friendship of the two men was at an end.

Bohr was later to make a dramatic escape from German-occupied Denmark and join Oppenheimer and the others at Los Alamos. The information that he communicated about his meeting with Heisenberg put the German scientist at the very top of General Groves's "hit list." What the drawing of the German heavy-water reactor should have told the Allied scientists was that the Germans were on the wrong track and several years behind in their research. What it actually communicated was the stark fact that the Germans had an active atomic-bomb research project in progress and it had to be stopped.

A variety of schemes were discussed involving the kidnapping or assassination of leading German scientists like Heisenberg. None of these schemes was ever carried out, though one nearly was.

In December 1944, Heisenberg went to Zurich, Switzerland—Switzerland was neutral during the war—to deliver a physics lecture. In the audience was an American OSS agent, with a pistol in his pocket and authority to kill the scientist if he thought necessary. The OSS, Office of Special Services, was the wartime precursor to the CIA, Central Intelligence Agency. The agent was Morris (Moe) Berg, one of the most colorful figures in the history of U.S.

Morris (Moe) Berg in his last season of baseball. An accomplished linguist and a lawyer, Berg retired from baseball in January 1942 and went to work on the staff of Nelson A. Rockefeller, who was then involved in international affairs.

intelligence. Berg had been a major league baseball catcher, with the reputation of being the smartest man in baseball. He was an extraordinary linguist, and when the war started he became a spy. Berg said that before he went to Switzerland he had been drilled in physics, to listen for certain things. If anything Heisenberg said convinced Berg the Germans were close to a bomb, it was his job to shoot him right there in the auditorium. It would certainly have been a suicide mission, for there would have been no way for Berg to escape.

Heisenberg's lecture was on an abstruse theory in physics that had nothing to do with building an atomic bomb, and which Berg himself did not understand at all. Berg later said that he was ready to shoot the scientist and damn the consequences if so much as a word suggested that Hitler had an atomic bomb.

Thomas Powers, who wrote a massive study of Heisenberg's participation in the German atomic program, wrote: "Berg went over this moment again and again in his mind for the rest of his life, evidence that it was desperately real to him. But the truth probably is that Heisenberg would have had to click his heels and announce with evil laughter the imminent annihilation of the Allies with atomic fury before Berg would have drawn his pistol."[4]

Berg trailed Heisenberg all over Zurich, and even contrived to attend a dinner party with him, and followed him back to his hotel, peppering him with leading questions. Heisenberg apparently never had any idea that the annoyingly talkative fellow, whom he took to be Swiss, was ready to kill him.

Surprisingly the United States did not mount a large-scale effort to actually find out how far Germany had gone toward developing an atomic bomb until the war was nearly over. In late 1943, General Groves authorized the formation of an intelligence unit named Alsos.

Alsos was under the command of Lieutenant Colonel Boris T. Pash. As the German armies began to be pushed back in late 1944, men from Alsos followed the advancing Allied armies trying to ferret out whatever information they could in the newly liberated territories. In the spring of 1945, Pash led his men across Germany to locate and seize any nuclear material that might exist and to hunt down and capture any German nuclear scientists who were still at large. The aim was twofold. There was a lingering fear that if the collapsing German Reich possessed any kind of nuclear weapons the desperate Hitler might use them somehow. The second aim was to keep any materials and scientists out of the hands of the Soviet troops who were rushing through Germany from the East. World War II in Europe was drawing rapidly to a close. The first rumblings of the cold war to come were already being heard.

Pash had information that the top German atomic scientists were in the resort town of Haigerloch in the Black Forest region. By late April the German front had broken and the French were moving ahead. Pash and his men risked and returned German fire and got through to Haigerloch before the French. Most of the scientists were there, along with what the Germans called a uranium "machine"—actually a small and rather primitive atomic pile. Heisenberg wasn't there, but he was located at a vacation cottage in Bavaria a few days later.

What Pash discovered was that the Germans didn't really have much of an atomic-weapons program. They were years behind the Manhattan Project, and there was no possibility that they could mount any sort of a last-ditch nuclear attack. This was what Pash called, with some justification, "probably the most significant single piece of military intelligence developed during the war." In the final years of the war Germany concentrated on building the V-1 and V-2 rockets, not atomic bombs.

After the war there was a good deal of speculation about why the German nuclear program had been so feeble. Had some of the German scientists actually sabotaged the program by overstressing the difficulties? Some later claimed that this is what had actually happened, but such claims may have been self-serving. Had German research just taken a wrong turn at a critical moment and had no time to recoup? No one really knows.

In the spring of 1945 it was quite clear that Germany was going to collapse before an atomic bomb could be successfully developed at Los Alamos. These facts were well known among the military men and scientists who controlled the Manhattan Project. Yet there was no thought of ending the project—if anything work went ahead more energetically than ever.

Chapter 6

THE ROAD TO TRINITY

BY EARLY 1944 A CRISIS had developed at Los Alamos. The difficulties in getting adequate quantities of fissionable material were staggering.

General Groves had taken an enormous gamble in building a half-billion-dollar secret factory, actually more like a small city, in Oak Ridge, Tennessee. The factory began operating in August 1943, but it kept breaking down. It was only producing tiny amounts of pure uranium 235. Oppenheimer was told he could count on enough uranium for just one bomb by mid-1945.

Groves had made a second gamble in building yet another secret city, this one near Hanford, Washington, to produce a second fissionable material, plutonium 239. Some 45,000 construction workers labored under harsh and primitive conditions to rush construction of the Hanford facility. By 1945 it was estimated that Hanford would produce enough plutonium for more than one bomb in the next few months.

There were actually two types of atomic bombs being developed at Los Alamos. The uranium bomb was long and thin and initially called "Thin Man" after Roosevelt. But the size of the bomb was cut down and the nickname changed to "Little Boy." The plutonium bomb was rounder and called "Fat Man" after Winston Churchill.

Everyone was absolutely convinced that a uranium bomb detonated by the gun method would work. But early in 1944 it became increasingly apparent that the gun method would not work with plutonium. That meant that Neddermeyer's implosion method would be used. However, the technology of the plutonium bomb was much newer and more complicated. It absolutely had to be tested before it was used. And that meant that someplace in America had to be found to test the most potentially awesome weapon that the world had ever seen.

Finding a suitable place to test "the gadget" started in May 1944. The requirements for the site were strict. The area had to be relatively flat, both to minimize the effects of the terrain on the blast and to maximize the opportunities for a variety of experiments and observations. The weather in the region had to be basically good. The site had to be isolated from any centers of population, yet close enough to Los Alamos to allow for the easy movement of men and equipment.

A number of sites were considered and turned down for various reasons. One of them, in the California desert, had been used by General George Patton as a training ground. Groves called Patton "the most disagreeable man I ever met," and absolutely refused to talk to him about the site. In September an area called the Jornada del Muerto was finally settled on. Translated the name means "Journey of Death." The Jornada is a stretch of high desert lying between present-day Socorro, New Mexico, and El Paso, Texas. It is bounded by the San Andres and San Mateos mountains. The sandy soil supports only sparse vegetation, and while the winters are cool and mild, summer temperatures often reach well over 100°F (38°C). In the early 1940s the region had only a few scattered sheep and cattle ranches. Once the war started the federal government leased several hundred square miles to be used for test bombing, and this became the Alamogordo Bombing Range.

Construction on the site was in full swing by November. The construction company in charge of the work didn't know what they were working on. A supervisor recalled, "You just did the job required. You didn't go ask questions or worry about money."[1] The fact that they were building enormous concrete bunkers and reinforced steel towers led the construction workers to conclude that whatever the area was going to be used for it had to do with high explosives. They had no idea what sort of explosives these might be.

At first the scientists were so unsure that the bomb would work that they proposed putting it inside an enormous steel container. If the bomb worked then the container would be vaporized instantly. If it didn't whatever blast there was would be contained and the costly plutonium could be recovered. When it was finally built, the container, called Jumbo, weighed 214 tons and had 15-inch (38-centimeter)-thick walls of banded steel. Getting the enormous contraption to the test site was one of the hardest parts of the construction. It was the heaviest single object ever moved by railroad.

Jumbo arrived at the test site in early April 1945, but by that time those in charge decided that it wouldn't be needed after all. Confidence in the implosion system had increased greatly. Later Groves actually tried to have the thing blown up with conventional explosives so that congressional investigators would not begin asking questions about why so much money was spent on something that was never used. All they ever managed to do is blow the ends out of it—the remains of Jumbo are still in the desert.[2]

The site itself came to be called Trinity—though no one is exactly sure why. A number of suggestions have been advanced. The most probable is that Oppenheimer named the site. Oppenheimer had a great interest in the Hindu religion. The Hindu concept of Trinity consists of Brahma, the Creator; Vishnu, the Preserver; and Shiva, the Destroyer. For Hindus, whatever exists in the universe is never destroyed. It is simply transformed. The cycle of life is such that if one part dies, another one is created from it. Oppenheimer himself, however, never confirmed this version of the naming of Trinity.

The pressures at Los Alamos during late 1944 and 1945 were extraordinarily heavy, and they began to take their toll—particularly on Oppenheimer. He was always thin, but now he became nearly skeletal. He had tried to smoke a pipe but was now back to chain-smoking five packs of cigarettes a day. That was considered excessive even though the full dangers of smoking were not recognized in 1944. He had so much trouble sleeping that he was taking powerful sleeping pills practically every night. But he didn't slacken his frenetic work schedule, and the doubts and fears that constantly assailed him, he kept to himself.

A bright spot in a dark time at Los Alamos was the arrival of Niels Bohr. "They didn't need my help in making the atom bomb," Bohr later told a friend. Bohr did get an office at Los Alamos, and he participated in many of the discussions, offering solutions to some of the technical problems to be solved. But his main contribution was psychological, not scientific.

Next to Einstein, Niels Bohr was the most respected physicist in the world. Many of those at Los Alamos had been his associates and students. Oppie was among his greatest admirers.

For purposes of security Bohr was given the name Nicholas Baker, and many called him "Uncle Nick." "Somehow he seemed the embodiment of wisdom," recalled mathematician Stanislaw M. Ulam. "If Bohr was there, it would have to work," said engineer Bernard J. O'Keefe. "He made the enterprise, which often looked so macabre, seem hopeful," Oppenheimer later recalled.[3]

Bohr had a vision beyond the war. He wanted to see that the power being unleashed at Los Alamos would be used for good, not evil, purposes. He hoped that after the war the use of nuclear power could be turned over to international control. He wanted to meet with Roosevelt and Churchill and convince them that they should tell Russia's leader, Joseph Stalin, about the bomb quickly and make an offer to share control. Bohr knew that there was no way to keep the nuclear secrets secret forever, or even for very long. Openness, he believed, would be the only way to avoid polarization between the two great powers and avoid a future arms race.

In Washington, Bohr got the impression that he was being encouraged to meet with Churchill and "explore ways for achieving proper safeguards in relation to X." *X* being, of course, the atomic bomb. Elated, Bohr went to London

Niels Bohr,
whose research
started it all

in March, but the reception he got from Churchill was any-thing but friendly. Churchill was busy planning for the D Day invasion of Normandy—only three weeks away. He was distracted and in a bad mood. He thought Bohr's ideas were dangerously naive, and he told him so.

Bohr did not give up, and back in Washington he got a friendlier reception from Roosevelt. The president, who had heard all about the disastrous meeting with Churchill, laughed and said Winston could be difficult, particularly when he was in a bad mood. He appeared to agree that the Russian dictator should be approached, and said that he would take the matter up with Churchill once again when the two met in Quebec in September.

But in Quebec it appears that Churchill convinced Roosevelt. They signed an agreement that after the war atomic energy should be kept strictly in the hands of the United States and Britain.

Churchill had become so hostile to Bohr that he began to regard him as downright dangerous and wanted him watched to make sure that he did not turn over any atomic secrets to the Russians. He knew that Bohr had received an invitation to come to Russia from his old friend the Russian physicist Peter Kapitza. Bohr had turned down the invitation—and had immediately reported it to the British secret service. Churchill wrote: "The President and I are much worried about Professor Bohr. How did he come into this business? . . . It seems to me Bohr ought to be confined or at any rate made to see that he is very near the edge of mortal crimes. . . . I do not like it at all."

On March 15, 1945, President Roosevelt was told that the atomic bomb would probably be ready for testing by summer.

In April, Oak Ridge had finally produced enough uranium 235 for a single bomb. The material was shipped to Los Alamos where physicist Rudolf Peierls assembled the bomb—by hand.

At about the same time those working on an implosion bomb had made impressive strides, and Oppenheimer was able to send Groves the cheering news that they were just about ready.

Then on April 12, Franklin Delano Roosevelt died of a massive cerebral hemorrhage while vacationing at Warm Springs, Georgia. He was in the 63rd year of his life and had served his nation as president for 13 years—more than any other president before or since. Roosevelt had been in failing health for months, but this was known only to his closest associates. The nation was stunned.

On April 15 everybody at Los Alamos gathered at the theater where Oppenheimer spoke briefly:

"When, three days ago, the world had word of the death of President Roosevelt, many wept who are unaccustomed to tears, many men and women, little enough accustomed to prayer, prayed to God. Many of us looked with deep trouble to the future; many of us felt less certain that our works would be to a good end; and all of us were reminded of how precious a thing human greatness is.

"We have been living through years of great evil, and of great terror. Roosevelt has been our president, our commander in chief and, in an old and unperverted sense, our leader. All over the world men have looked to him for guidance, and have seen symbolized in him their hope that the evils of this time would not be repeated; that the terrible sacrifices which have been made, and those that are still to be made, would lead to a world more fit for human habitation.

"In the Hindu scripture, in the Bhagavad Gita, it says 'Man is a creature whose substance is faith. What faith is, he is.' The faith of Roosevelt is one that is shared by millions of men and women in every country of the world. For this reason it is possible to maintain the hope, for this reason it is right that we should dedicate ourselves to the hope, that his good works will not have ended with his death."[4]

If Roosevelt could inspire, so could Oppenheimer. This was Oppie at his best.

Chapter 7

TESTING "THE GADGET"

VICE PRESIDENT HARRY S TRUMAN took the oath of office at 7:09 P.M. on April 12, 1945. The ceremony lasted a minute. About an hour later he was told about the atomic bomb.

Roosevelt had been widely loved by many Americans and deeply hated by some—but he had led the nation through the Great Depression and World War II. He was an immense presence. Truman was barely known. He had been an undistinguished senator from Missouri and regarded as little more than a figurehead. He had never been close to Roosevelt, and he had never expected to become president. Although he had a general idea that there was a large secret war project being conducted, he had no clear idea of what it was.

Roosevelt's secretary of war, Henry W. Stimson, took the new president aside on "a most urgent matter" and briefly sketched an "immense project" that would give the nation "a new explosive of almost unbelievable power."

Truman was still puzzled, and the next day James F. "Jimmy" Byrnes told him a bit more. Byrnes was the ultimate Washington insider. He had been a congressman, senator, supreme court justice, and under Roosevelt during the war he was sometimes called "assistant president." Byrnes held a variety of posts in the Roosevelt administration and in many ways ran domestic policy while the president took care of the war. He had expected to be Roosevelt's vice-presidential choice, but he was a conservative South Carolina Democrat and he was dropped in favor of the virtually unknown Truman—a moderate Democrat from a border state. Putting it as mildly as possible, Byrnes said he was "disappointed," and retired to private life. Byrnes was one of a handful of men to whom Roosevelt had confided the story of the Manhattan Project.

Byrnes related some of what he knew to Truman along with the observation that possession of such a weapon would give the United States tremendous influence in the postwar world. Truman quickly appointed Byrnes secretary of state.

As a senator, Truman had been aware that huge sums of money were going into a secret military project. When he tried to probe deeper he was sternly informed that the project was too secret to tell him about. He didn't learn any more as vice president. And it was still over a week after he had actually become president before General Groves was called in to provide a full briefing about the Manhattan Project and where the research stood.

Events were moving very rapidly now. On the evening of May 8, 1945, Dwight D. Eisenhower, the Supreme Allied Commander, went on the radio to announce that Germany had surrendered, and the war in Europe was over. It was V-E Day, Victory in Europe Day, and in America spontaneous celebrations erupted everywhere.

The Manhattan Project had been started to beat Hitler's Third Reich. Now Hitler was dead and the Third Reich had fallen. Yet no one in Washington and very few at Los Alamos seriously considered stopping the project at this point, just a few months before it could be successfully completed.

There was still the war in Asia. The Japanese were clearly going to be defeated. With the war in Europe at an end the Allies could focus all their might on Japan, and the inevitable end would come sooner rather than later. But the Japanese had shown themselves to be extraordinarily tenacious fighters, unwilling to surrender, even in the face of what appeared to be overwhelming odds. In the United States they were generally regarded as fanatics. What would be the cost in American lives of defeating Japan?

And then there were the Russians. The Soviet Union had rebounded incredibly from invasion and near defeat by Germany. Russian dictator Joseph Stalin was making increasingly aggressive moves in Eastern Europe, and Britain and the United States believed that he was violating wartime agreements about the future of Europe. If the Soviets joined the war against Japan then the West might have to trade away even more in Europe.

The "Big Three"—Stalin, Churchill, and Truman—had agreed to meet on July 15 for several days in Potsdam, a suburb of Berlin, to discuss the future of Europe and the course of the war in Asia. Byrnes and others believed that if Truman, an accidental president with absolutely no international negotiating experience, could have news of a successful atomic-bomb test in his pocket this would increase his confidence and strengthen his negotiating position enormously. Groves set the target date for the test on July 16, subject to the vagaries of the weather.

Mid-July was not an ideal time, for in mid-July temperatures at the Trinity site were often well over 100°F (38°C) and severe thunderstorms were common. Oppenheimer wired Washington in makeshift code: ANY TIME AFTER THE 15TH WOULD BE A GOOD TIME FOR OUR FISHING TRIP. BECAUSE WE ARE NOT CERTAIN OF THE WEATHER WE MAY BE DELAYED SEVERAL DAYS.[1]

The weather wasn't the only problem. A sufficient quantity of plutonium did not arrive from Hanford until May 31. Nobody at Los Alamos had ever seen the material before. Up to that point it was all theory. The bomb existed only in the notes and blackboard calculations of the scientists. The plutonium arrived as a syrupy nitrate that had to be purified and transformed into metal. To make the core of the bomb, 13½ pounds (6 kilograms) of the metal had to be shaped into two identical and absolutely smooth spheres.

There were all sorts of last-minute problems. And there was no time to fix them elegantly. At one point scientists were reduced to grinding the surface of the plutonium spheres with dental drills. This was just one of many hurried improvisations that had to be employed, and no one was absolutely sure that the improvisations would work. At Los Alamos this bit of doggerel was making the rounds:

From this crude lab that spawned a dud
Their necks to Truman's ax uncurled
Lo, the embattled savants stood
And fired a flop heard 'round the world.[2]

The pressure was enormous. In a letter to Eleanor Roosevelt in 1950, Oppenheimer recalled one incident shortly before the test:

"Everyone rushed out to stare at a bright object in the sky through binoculars or whatever else they could find. The nearby air base told them that there were no interceptors that could get within range of the unknown object.

"Our director of personnel was an astronomer and a man of some human wisdom; and he finally came to my office and asked whether we would stop trying to shoot down Venus. I tell the story only to indicate that even a group of scientists is not proof against the errors of suggestion and hysteria."[3]

The plutonium core was taken to Trinity on July 12. It was in a case studded with rubber bumpers and rode in the backseat of an army sedan like a distinguished visitor, a carload of armed guards clearing the way ahead and another of assembly specialists bringing up the rear. Preliminary assembly was done on a table in an old ranch house at the site. The house had been meticulously vacuumed and its windows sealed with tape to protect against dust.

On July 13 the core was then driven to the base of the 100-foot (30-meter) tower at Trinity site for final assembly. There was a moment of panic when the core refused to click into place. The operation had been rehearsed a hundred times, but something was wrong. The heat had expanded the plutonium core. After a few minutes it had cooled down and clicked into place perfectly. The gadget was then hoisted to the top of the tower with a power winch.

On the night of July 15 several bus and carloads of VIP observers began to arrive. They were to watch the test from Compania Hill about 20 miles (32 kilometers) northwest

The world's first atomic bomb being readied for transport to the Trinity site, in Alamogordo, New Mexico

of Trinity. All airports within 100 miles (161 kilometers) were told to ban aircraft from the area.

Among the observers was William Laurence, the science reporter for the *New York Times*, and the only reporter to witness the test. He was sworn to secrecy. He had even prepared several cover stories already filed with the *Times* in case something went seriously wrong and had to be explained away. In one story he wrote the obituaries of people who might have been killed in the blast, including his own. In this version the people were supposed to have died as the result of a freak explosion at Oppenheimer's ranch.

While the VIPs were at what was assumed to be a safe distance of 20 miles (32 kilometers), there were much closer observation points. Earth-sheltered bunkers with concrete slab roofs supported by oak beams thicker than railroad ties were located 5.7 miles (9 kilometers) from ground zero. Several of them held lights, cameras, and various scientific instruments. One of them called South 10,000 was to serve as the control bunker for the test. Another, 5 miles (8 kilometers) farther south, was Base Camp where the majority of those who were actually involved in the atomic-bomb test had been housed, and from where they would watch the events unfold.

Groves was concerned about possible saboteurs. The Japanese might launch a parachute assault. He ordered a team headed by explosives expert George Kistiakowsky to guard the tower before the scheduled test. A furious "Kisty" spent the night perched on the tower. He didn't think the precaution was necessary. Below, soldiers with flashlights and submachine guns patrolled ground zero.

The test was scheduled for 4 A.M., but the weather turned bad as thunderstorms moved in. "What the hell is wrong with the weather," Groves shouted. At 2 A.M. Groves and Oppenheimer drove from their observation post at South 10,000 to a spot much nearer the tower where they resumed waiting, worrying, and trying to outguess the weather. At 2:30 the storm hit ground zero and knocked out one of the searchlights illuminating the tower. There was an irrational fear that lightning might actually set the bomb off. The 4 A.M. time was dropped and the test was rescheduled for 5:30, weather permitting.

Shortly after three o'clock the rain stopped. About 4 A.M. the cloud cover broke and the wind began to die down. Meteorologists who had been monitoring conditions every 15 minutes predicted that calm conditions would hold for at least the next two hours. At approximately 5 A.M. the arming party under Kistiakowsky at the tower checked the electrical connections, threw the final switches, and drove their jeeps quickly 5 miles (8 kilometers) to the control bunker at South 10,000. By that time Groves had driven off to join the high-ranking scientists from Los Alamos and other VIPs who were 20 miles (32 kilometers) from ground zero. Oppenheimer remained at the South 10,000 bunker, which was now the nerve center for the test.

The countdown began at zero minus 20 minutes.

A warning rocket that was supposed to have fired as a two-minute warning fizzled. The one-minute warning rocket and siren went off as planned.

At 5:29 A.M. Sam Allison, a University of Chicago physicist who had been conducting the countdown, yelled "Zero."

Nothing happened. Then suddenly the sky ignited. The flash was seen in three states. It lit up the sky like the sun, throwing out a multicolored cloud that surged 38,000 feet

*The mushroom cloud of the first atomic bomb.
Temperatures near the site of the explosion reached
100 million degrees, windows 125 miles (201 km) away
were shattered, and the sky was lit with a brightness
many times that of ordinary sunlight.*

(11,582 meters) into the atmosphere in about seven minutes. For over an hour the immediate area lay under a pall of smoke. The heat at the center of the blast approximated that of the center of the sun, and the light was brighter than 20 suns. Where the fireball touched the ground it created a crater half a mile across, fusing the sand into a greenish gray glass. Every living thing within the radius of a mile was annihilated—plants, snakes, ground squirrels, lizards, even the ants.

The reactions of those who witnessed the event ranged from awe to horror to relief and joy. But undoubtedly the most relieved man at that moment was physicist Kenneth T. Bainbridge. If the bomb had not gone off it would have been his task to climb the test tower alone and find out what had gone wrong—and possibly set the thing off by accident. He grabbed Oppenheimer's hand and shook it vigorously and said: "Oppie, now we're all sons of bitches!"

The test had been a complete success, said by Oppenheimer to be "technically sweet." The gadget was still a secret and destined to remain one for another month. However, an event of this magnitude could not be kept completely secret. Lots of people who had no idea what was going on and had not been sworn to secrecy saw the light and felt the shock waves. Almost immediately an official statement was issued:

"Several inquiries have been received concerning a heavy explosion which occurred on the Alamogordo Air Base reservation this morning.

"A remotely located ammunition magazine containing a considerable amount of high explosives and pyrotechnics exploded.

Dr. Oppenheimer and General Groves pose for the photographers at ground zero. In front of them is the partial remains of the tower that supported the bomb.

"There was no loss of life or injury to anyone, and the property damage outside of the explosives magazine itself was negligible.

"Weather conditions affecting the content of gas shells exploded by the blast may make it desirable for the army to evacuate temporarily a few civilians from their homes."[4]

The War Department pressured local newspapers not to use any background information, add no details, and speculate about no other explanations. Most of them complied. A cub reporter for a Chicago newspaper got a call from a man who had been traveling through the area and told her, in great detail, about the crash of a huge meteorite. She wrote a short article about it. The next day she found herself being grilled by FBI agents and promised to write no more about "the meteorite."

In Potsdam, President Truman got word of the successful atomic-bomb test. He was sorely in need of good news because he hated the trip. The accommodations were terrible and he was feeling very unsure of himself. The first news arrived on the evening of July 16 in the form of a coded message that read in part: "Operated this morning. Diagnosis not yet complete . . . ."

More details arrived on July 21 in a letter from General Groves that was dispatched by special courier plane. It said, in part: "The test was successful beyond the most optimistic expectations of anyone."

The president was tremendously pepped up by the news. Churchill noticed the change immediately and when he heard Groves's report he knew why. At a formal meeting with the Soviets Harry Truman was a different man. Churchill wrote: "He told the Russians just where they got on and off and generally bossed the whole meeting."

Truman arrived at Potsdam eager to persuade the Soviets to enter the war with the United States and Britain against Japan. That no longer seemed like an urgent issue. The possibility of international control of atomic energy was a live issue before the test—now it was dead. Truman had planned to formally tell Stalin about the bomb's existence; now there was a new plan. He was going to casually mention the subject to the Soviet premier after the formal sessions had ended.

The scene was carefully rehearsed. At the end of the formal conference, at about 7:30 P.M., Truman walked around the circular conference table and up to Stalin and his interpreter. He said in a rather offhand manner that the United States "had a new weapon of unusual destructive force."

In his memoirs Truman recorded: "The Russian premier showed no special interest. All he said was that he was glad to hear it and hoped we would 'make good use of it against the Japanese.'"

Both Truman and Churchill were delighted. They thought that they had fooled Stalin, that he had not realized the importance of what he had been told.

Stalin had not been fooled. He did not react, and was not more curious about Truman's strange remark because he already knew what it meant.

Chapter 8

SPIES

THERE WAS NO SINGLE BIG SECRET to the atomic bomb that could be stolen by a spy. There was no single formula or set of blueprints that would automatically give a nation the ability to build the bomb. All of the basic science needed for an atomic bomb had been developed before the war and was well known among the international community of physicists. Any technically advanced nation willing and able to commit sufficient resources to the program could have developed its own A-bomb.

There are, however, many, many small secrets. Even with the basic knowledge there were a huge number of theoretical and technical problems that had to be solved before a practical A-bomb could be produced. Answers to any of these smaller questions would be enormously valuable to any nation seeking to make its own bomb quickly. Their own researchers could be pointed in the right direction and could avoid time-consuming and expensive blind alleys.

It was not surprising that the United States was the first nation in the world to develop an atomic bomb. In 1940 the United States was the richest country in the world. It was the only major industrialized country that was not already being consumed by the war. In addition to a large body of homegrown scientists, the United States had become a refuge for many of the world's best scientists. Most of these refugee scientists had compelling reasons to see that the bomb was developed in the United States rather than Germany.

Only the United States could bring together the largest concentration of scientific talent in the world and provide them with nearly unlimited resources. That was the Manhattan Project.

From the start there was a great concern for security. The obvious fear was, of course, that the project would be penetrated by German, and to a lesser extent Japanese, spies. That fear proved to be unfounded.

There was also a fear that the project would be penetrated by spies for the Soviet Union. While the Soviets were allies during the war they were not trusted friends as were the British. Before the war there was enormous hostility between the United States and the Soviets. Many in America believed that Stalin was a greater threat than Hitler. Many more had hoped that the Russians and the Germans would destroy each other in the war and America would never have to become involved. Even during the war many Americans assumed that as soon as the fighting stopped the U.S.-Soviet rivalry would begin again in earnest.

But there were also those—a minority, but by no means a lunatic fringe—who were greatly attracted to the Soviet Union's Communist ideology. The United States had not really recovered from the Great Depression and the Communist promise of economic equality had tremendous appeal. Though Hitler and Stalin had signed a short-lived nonaggression pact (which the Germans broke in 1939), Communists had been among the earliest, most vigorous, and bravest opponents of the Nazis.

In the Spanish Civil War (1936–1939), Communists and other leftists from many countries fought on the side of the Republican government, which had been threatened by an insurgency led by General Francisco Franco and strongly backed by the Nazis and the Italian Fascists. The United States and other Allied countries declared "neutrality," which effectively guaranteed the victory of the Franco forces. In Spain the Germans were able to gain some military experience that was later put to use in World War II. Some felt that by their inaction the Allies had emboldened the Nazis to ever more aggressive actions.

After Hitler broke the nonaggression pact and attacked the Soviet Union, the savagery was unparalleled. Over 20 million Russians died during the war. Despite almost universal predictions that the Soviet Union would collapse, the Soviets stopped the German advance and turned the tide of the war.

So in addition to the appeal that communism held there was the fact that the Soviets were allies during the war— heroic allies.

The subject of Soviet atomic spies has been one of the most extensively researched and hotly debated areas in the history of the development of the bomb. Yet even now, well over half a century after the Manhattan Project ended, new information is being revealed, and much about it still remains unknown.

Probably the most effective Soviet spy at Los Alamos was the German émigré scientist Klaus Fuchs. Fuchs, the son of a Lutheran minister, had become a dedicated Communist in Germany. When Hitler rose to power, Fuchs fled to Britain where he became a naturalized citizen. A talented scientist, he obtained a doctorate in science and mathematics and a position at Birmingham University.

Fuchs was actually working in atomic research, and in November 1943 he, along with several other British scientists, boarded a troopship for the United States in order to participate in the biggest atomic research project in the world.

He first went to New York City, where he worked with a group at Columbia University on uranium separation and passed information along to his contact, a man named Harry Gold. He later moved on to the center of research, Los Alamos.

At Los Alamos, Klaus Fuchs fit right in. He was bright, hardworking, efficient, and very helpful. He seemed to enjoy mountain climbing, skiing, and driving around the countryside, at dangerously high speeds, in his battered blue Buick convertible. He was extremely quiet and was given the nickname "Penny-in-the-slot Fuchs" because he seemed to talk only when compelled to. Still he was popular, and got on so well with the children of the married scientists he became a favorite baby-sitter.[1]

Los Alamos scientists held regular sessions in which they discussed the future of the A-bomb after the war. Many of them openly argued for giving the information to the Soviet Union. Niels Bohr was the most prominent among the scientists who held this view. Fuchs rarely even attended such sessions. He kept his political opinions to himself.

Klaus Fuchs did not have access to all of the Los Alamos information, but he had access to a great deal of it, and he regularly passed the information on to contact Harry Gold, whom he met on vacation trips to the East Coast. Shortly before the Trinity test Gold made a special trip to the Southwest to meet Fuchs in Santa Fe. All in all, Fuchs's contribution to the Soviet atomic-bomb effort was enormous.

It wasn't until late 1949 that Fuchs was identified. After he was arrested in Britain he confessed and named Gold as his contact. Gold confessed that on his trip to Santa Fe he also contacted another man, a draftsman from the Los Alamos workshop named David Greenglass, who gave him a small sketch. After his arrest Greenglass told of how he had been recruited for spy duty by his brother-in-law, Julius Rosenberg. Rosenberg and his wife, Ethel, were also arrested. While Gold and Greenglass cooperated with the FBI, the Rosenbergs refused to do so. They always maintained their innocence.

This set the stage for what was to become the most famous and most controversial spy trial in 20th century U.S. history. The Rosenbergs were dubbed the "Atomic Spies." The small sketch of what was called an implosion lens was termed "priceless" by the presiding judge. The general impression was that the Rosenbergs had given away the secret of the atomic bomb.

In fact, the drawing was rather crude and amateurish, and while Greenglass may have passed additional information to his brother-in-law, he was not a particularly knowledgeable or important part of the Los Alamos operation. Everything he could possibly have known would have already been turned over by the more well-placed and knowledgeable Fuchs.

Even before they began receiving substantial information from Fuchs, the Soviets had their own A-bomb pro-

Ethel and Julius Rosenberg

gram, though the United States was unaware of this. The program was headed by Igor Kurchatov, a very competent physicist. Kurchatov was known to his friends as "the Beard," because he sported a huge spade-shaped beard. There is no doubt that the Soviets would have developed their own nuclear weapons without the information they received from their spies. There is also no doubt that this information allowed them to possess nuclear weapons two to three years earlier than they otherwise might have.

After a sensational trial the Rosenbergs were convicted and sentenced to death. They were both executed at New York's Sing Sing prison on June 19, 1953.

For many years supporters of the Rosenbergs insisted that they were innocent, and that they had essentially been railroaded to their deaths in the period of anti-Communist hysteria that gripped America during the 1950s. However, in the years since the fall of the Soviet Union, evidence has emerged indicating beyond any reasonable doubt that Julius Rosenberg was indeed a Soviet agent.

But controversy has continued over their fate. Ethel Rosenberg's involvement was marginal at best. The information was given to the Soviets at a time when they were wartime allies, not enemies. Most of all, they had not given away the secret of the A-bomb, because there was no single secret. Klaus Fuchs had passed on far more valuable information, but he was tried in Britain, and given a 14-year prison sentence. With time off for good behavior he was released in 1954 and allowed to return to Communist East Germany where he became deputy director of a nuclear research institute. The contrast between the fate of the spies is stark. The anti-Communist atmosphere in Britain during the 1950s was far less inflamed than in the United States.

Klaus Fuchs, upon his release from prison, having served nine years of a fourteen-year sentence.

It has long been suspected that there were other Soviet spies at Los Alamos, but it wasn't until 1995 that information was revealed about yet another American atomic spy. In many ways he was the most remarkable of all.

In 1943 Ted Hall was a 17-year-old New Yorker, studying physics at Harvard University. He was approached by a man from Washington who told him "that there was this project that was doing quite important work and they needed more hands." Ted Hall asked about the work but was told only that it was very secret and that he shouldn't talk about it to anyone. Though he didn't know it at the time, he was being asked to join Robert Oppenheimer's project at Los Alamos.

Hall was about to turn 18 and thus would have been eligible for the draft. He was made to feel as if this secret work would be far more important to the war effort. So he agreed, and he arrived in New Mexico in January 1944— still without knowing what it was that he would be doing. At 18 he was probably the youngest member of the Los Alamos scientific staff.

Like many of his background and generation, Ted Hall had a great deal of sympathy for the Soviet Union. Even before he knew what sort of secret work he would be doing he considered the possibility of turning information over to the Soviets. Once he realized that he was working on an atomic bomb he was determined that was what he should do. But how to do it?

Unlike Klaus Fuchs or Julius Rosenberg, Hall did not have a longtime Communist background and never had any previous contact with Soviet officials. In mid-October 1944, Hall returned to New York from Los Alamos on a two-week vacation. Along with his former Harvard roommate, Saville Sax, Hall went looking for a Soviet agent to whom he could give atomic secrets. First they contacted organizations like the one that distributed Russian films, hoping to find someone who would listen to them. The Russians thought either that these kids were crazy or that this approach was really an FBI provocation. They wanted nothing to do with it.

Just a few days before he was scheduled to go back to New Mexico, Hall walked into the warehouse of Amtorg, a Soviet export-import business. He thought that some "nice businessman" might prove helpful. What he did not know was that Amtorg was really a front for Soviet spies. There he was given the name of Sergi Kurnakov, a journalist whose main job was spying. Kurnakov's father had been a

~~TOP SECRET~~

USSR

Ref. No: ████

Issued: ████ 25/4/1961 // ;

Copy No: 2C/4

DECISION TO MAINTAIN CONTACT WITH THEODORE HALL (1944)

From: NEW YORK

To: MOSCOW

No: 1585   12 Nov. 44

To VIKTOR.[i]

BEK[ii] visited Theodore HALL[TEODOR KhOLL],[iii] 19 years old, the son of a furrier. He is a graduate of HARVARD University. · As a talented physicist he was taken on for government work. He was a GYMNAST[FIZKUL'TURNIK][iv] and conducted work in the Steel Founders' Union.[a] 'According to BEK's account HALL has an exceptionally keen mind and a broad outlook, and is politically developed. At the present time H. is in charge of a group at "CAMP-2"[v] (SANTA-FE). H. handed over to BEK a report about the CAMP and named the key personnel employed on ENORMOUS.[vi] He decided to do this on the advice of his colleague Saville SAX[SAVIL SAKS],[vii] a GYMNAST living in TYRE.[viii] SAX's mother is a FELLOWCOUNTRYMAN[ZEMLYaK][ix] and works for RUSSIAN WAR RELIEF. With the aim of hastening a meeting with a competent person, H. on the following day sent a copy of the report by S. to the PLANT[ZAVOD].[x] ALEKSEJ[xi] received S. H. had to leave for CAMP-2 in two days' time. He[b] was compelled to make a decision quickly. Jointly with MAJ[MAJ],[xii] he gave BEK consent to feel out H., to assure him that everything was in order and to arrange liaison with him. H. left his photograph and came to an understanding with BEK about a place for meeting him. BEK met S. [1 group garbled] our automobile. We consider it expedient to maintain liaison with H. [1 group unidentified] through S. and not to bring in anybody else. MAJ has no objection to this. We shall send the details by post.

No. 897   [Signature missing]

This CIA document shows the deciphered cable that prompted them to begin files on both Ted Hall and Saville Sax. When the U.S. Army codebreakers unscrambled the cable, they had proof that Hall and Sax had been recruited to spy, and they undoubtedly soon knew that Hall in particular had access to classified information.

scientist, and so when Hall started talking Kurnakov understood what was being described and could hardly believe his good fortune. Kurnakov asked for proof that Hall was who he claimed to be. The young man came prepared. He handed Kurnakov a folder containing a report that he had written on Los Alamos and a list of all the scientists working there. Ted Hall had become an atomic spy, and he provided his own courier, his friend Saville Sax. Hall and Sax never took any money from the Russians. When money was offered Hall was insulted.[2]

Ted Hall was only a junior scientist at Los Alamos, though he did work on some critical areas in A-bomb construction. He witnessed the Trinity explosion as part of a team whose job it would be to evacuate nearby farms and ranches if anything went wrong.

At this time it is still quite impossible to determine how vital Ted Hall's information was to the Soviets. Klaus Fuchs was in a far more favorable position to obtain critical data. But if nothing else, Hall turned over information that confirmed what was being supplied by Fuchs and perhaps others. In espionage, confirmation is extremely important. Information received from a single agent can be wrong or deliberate misinformation. But if the same information is coming from several sources one can have more confidence in it.

The Soviets were committing a large portion of their scarce resources to their own A-bomb project. They were doing it to match what they perceived as an American threat, and they were using techniques from Los Alamos. It was a huge gamble and they had to be right.

Hall passed his information on to Sax who then gave it to the Russians. The two young men were inexperienced and clumsy spies, and in retrospect it seems amazing that they weren't caught. Later Ted was assigned a more seasoned contact, a woman named Lona Cohen. The result was an incident that became a classic in the history of Soviet espionage stories.

Lona was to meet Ted on the campus of the University of New Mexico in Albuquerque. Ted passed her some papers and she hustled back to the boardinghouse where her bags were already packed. She hid the papers under some tissues in a Kleenex box and headed for the train station.

It turned out to be a very bad moment. The bomb had been dropped on Japan, and President Truman told the world about the A-bomb. For the first time the censorship and secrecy that had surrounded Los Alamos had been lifted, and the train station was full of police, FBI, and army intelligence agents. Everyone getting on the train was being searched and questioned.

Lona Cohen transformed herself into the image of a confused and slightly ditzy woman, who had misplaced her train ticket and was obviously a threat to no one. She began to search her purse frantically, and even got one of the policemen to help her. Then she actually handed the Kleenex box to a policeman while she continued to look for the lost ticket and answer questions in a rather confused manner. Finally she found the ticket and started to walk away and the policeman had to remind her to take the Kleenex box. If he had looked inside both she and Ted Hall might have wound up in the electric chair.[3]

After Los Alamos closed down Ted enrolled in the University of Chicago, where many of the Los Alamos veterans like Teller and Fermi had gathered, and he pursued a doctorate in physics. He regularly walked by Stagg Field, where Enrico Fermi had conducted his critical chain reaction experiment.

Ted married a woman who shared his radical politics, and to whom he confided the story of his experiences as a spy. She was sympathetic but wanted him to abandon a clandestine life and openly take part in left-wing politics. One thing a Soviet spy could not do was draw attention to himself by espousing pro-Soviet positions.

But at the end of August 1948, Ted got a message from his old friend Savy Sax—the Soviets wanted him back. Just exactly what happened is not clear, though Ted apparently did rejoin the Soviet espionage service for a while. He began dressing like a spy—that meant he had to dress like everyone else. Spies are not supposed to be noticed. He had to wear a hat. Ted hated hats, but he bought a fedora. Savy, who was a notoriously eccentric dresser, had to buy a whole new wardrobe, from a suit to an overcoat and, of course, the required fedora. They also started wearing male jewelry—tie clips with golf clubs and racehorses. The Soviets used them as recognition signals for agents who had never seen one another before. But they were totally alien to Ted Hall and Saville Sax.[4]

Just what Ted Hall could have offered the Soviets at this time is unknown. He was no longer engaged in classified work. He may have passed on information obtained from two possible Soviet agents still known only as Anta and Aden. But even this is unclear. There may have been a New York meeting with Soviet master spy Colonel Rudolf Abel, who tried to persuade Ted to continue as an agent. Ted wavered, but his wife was pregnant and she was frightened. Ultimately he quit. His Soviet contacts apparently wished him well in his new life.

Ted switched from nuclear physics to biophysics. In time he and his family moved to Britain where he worked at Cambridge University's famous Cavendish laboratory and where he made some genuinely important scientific contributions.

It is not that Ted Hall was never suspected of being a spy. He very definitely was. At one point both he and Sax were intensively questioned by the FBI. They became so worried that they thought of fleeing to the Soviet Embassy dressed as women. Ted's wife shot that idea down saying that they could never fool anybody wearing high heels.

At that time a lot of people were suspected of being spies and questioned. Even if some FBI agents were convinced that the young scientist had been an important atomic spy they couldn't prove it. The case went onto the back burner, and while never closed, it was generally forgotten as the Cold War hysteria died down.

Savy Sax became an assistant professor of literature at Southern Illinois University. He died of a heart attack in 1980. In the years before his death he talked quite freely of having been a Soviet spy. He had always been regarded as something of an eccentric so people either didn't believe him or by that time, simply didn't care.

After the fall of the Soviet Union more and more information about intelligence-gathering activities began to filter out. By 1995, Ted Hall's name became public for the first time. There was a brief burst of publicity, some of it unsympathetic. One British newspaper suggested that he deserved the same fate as the Rosenbergs. But his friends and colleagues stood by him and the paper in Cambridge where he lived labeled him a "GREAT GUY ABSOLUTELY DEVOTED TO HIS SCIENCE."

Ted Hall was in poor health and virtually everyone who was directly connected to his Los Alamos activities was dead. There was no real danger that he would ever be prosecuted. So he began telling his side of the story. Hall did not regret what he had done. In fact, he was rather proud of it. When journalists Joseph Albright and Marcia Kunstel interviewed him for their book, *Bombshell: The Secret Story of America's Unknown Atomic Spy Conspiracy*, he presented them with a carefully worded justification. In part it read:

"In 1944 I was 19 years old—immature, inexperienced and far too sure of myself. I recognize that I could easily have been wrong in my judgment of what was necessary, and that I was indeed mistaken about some things, in particular my view of the nature of the Soviet state. The world has moved on a lot since then and certainly so have I. But in essence, from the perspective of my 71 years, I still think that brash youth had the right end of the stick. I am no longer that person, but I am by no means ashamed of him."[5]

Albright and Kunstel conclude: "No formal judgment is likely to close the case of Theodore Hall. Even on the scales of history, it is hard to weigh the consequences of putting American atomic research in the hands of the Soviet Union in the mid-1940s. There is no question that an arms race quickly followed, but so did a balance of power. Brushfires and regional wars flared, but no third world war. . . . What no one will ever know is if the bomb would have demolished other cities and peoples, had America managed to monopolize it for a decade longer."[6]

Chapter 9

AFTER TRINITY

THE MANHATTAN PROJECT ESSENTIALLY ENDED on July 16, 1945, after the successful test of the plutonium atomic bomb. There were still months of intensive scientific work to be done at Los Alamos, but the real action had moved elsewhere. The Manhattan Project had not been an ordinary scientific project aimed at experimenting with the principles of physics. The aim had been to build the deadliest weapon the world had ever seen in order to win a war.

Germany was finished, but the Japanese fought on. There was never any doubt among the scientists, military personnel, and politicians who were involved with the project that the bomb was going to be used on Japan if it did not surrender immediately and unconditionally. Japan had a small atomic bomb project of its own, but there was no possibility that the Japanese could have developed a bomb that could have been used in the war.

As the Trinity test was being planned, so too was the nuclear bombing of Japan. After Trinity the center of operations had effectively shifted to the island of Tinian, part of the Marshall Islands chain in the Pacific south of Japan. The little island had been transformed into the world's largest air base. Sometimes nearly a thousand B-29s took off in 15-second intervals from six 10-lane runways to bomb targets in Japan.

These bombing raids had been particularly devastating to Japanese cities, where houses were often built from light wood and rice paper and were consumed, along with their inhabitants, in the firestorms started by the bombs. The saturation bombings had been so successful that air force planners had trouble picking a target city for the first atomic bomb because so many Japanese cities had been effectively destroyed already. During the summer of 1945 the planners did manage to draw up a list of potential targets for the new weapon—Hiroshima, Kokura, Niigata, and Nagasaki. Hiroshima was thought to be a particularly attractive target because it had a large military depot, an industrial area, and was surrounded by hills, which would tend to focus the power of the blast. It was also the only one of the potential target cities that did not contain Allied prisoner-of-war camps. Hiroshima was at the top of the list.

On July 26, even before he returned from his meeting with Churchill and Stalin, President Truman issued what was called the Potsdam Declaration on behalf of himself, the president of Nationalist China, and the prime minister of Great Britain. It was a call for the unconditional surrender of Japan. This was not something to be negotiated— this was an ultimatum. "There are no alternatives. We shall brook no delay. . . . We call upon the government of Japan to proclaim now the unconditional surrender of all Japanese armed forces . . . the alternative for Japan is prompt and utter destruction."[1]

There was no mention of an atomic bomb, but the threat of "utter destruction" was ominous. On the same day that Truman issued his ultimatum, the U.S.S. *Indianapolis* dropped anchor a thousand yards off Tinian Harbor and unloaded the uranium 235 core for the Little Boy bomb that was to be dropped on Hiroshima. In a terrible irony, just four days later the *Indianapolis* was torpedoed by a Japanese submarine. It sank in 12 minutes. Of her 1,196-man crew, only 315 were rescued. More than twice that number had survived the sinking, but it was some 85 hours before they were spotted and rescued. There were few life-boats, and the majority of the survivors who were being kept afloat by life jackets gathered in clusters. They were blinded and crazed by the sun's glare from the oil slick and were picked off by sharks, which had gathered at the scene. It was one of the most gruesome episodes of the war.

As was expected, the Japanese rejected the Potsdam Declaration and so the plan to drop an atomic bomb on Japan continued relentlessly forward. In later years there was a good deal made of "the decision to drop the bomb." In reality, by the summer of 1945, that decision had already been made.

The plan was first to drop the reliable Little Boy uranium bomb. That would be followed by dropping the plutonium-based Fat Man on a second target, and plans called for the production and use of as many plutonium bombs as necessary to bring about the surrender of Japan. More and more bomb-making material was arriving at Tinian every day.

B-29s had already been modified to carry the new weapon. Crews had been chosen and specially trained, though they were not told, until the very last minute, what sort of weapon they were going to drop.

Truman never questioned whether the bomb should be used, and Churchill recalled that the use of the bomb "was never an issue." Some of the scientists who had worked at Los Alamos had strong reservations—but not Oppenheimer. Groves was all for the bombing, though some other military leaders were less enthusiastic because they thought that conventional bombing would do the job of bringing Japan to its knees. All objections to the use of the atomic bomb against Japan were simply swept aside by the momentum that had already been built up.

On August 4, 1945, the commander of the air force bomb-delivery team on Tinian called his men together to finally brief them on their mission. He said, "The bomb you are going to drop is something new in the history of warfare. It is the most destructive weapon ever produced. We think it will knock out almost everything within a 3-mile (5-kilometer) radius."

This introduction was to be followed by a brief film of the Trinity blast. Something went wrong and the projection camera began chewing up the film. To fill in, Captain William "Deke" Parsons, one of Groves's deputies, supplied a vivid word picture that left the men stunned. Even at this late date he avoided using the words *atomic* or *nuclear,* though he did warn the pilots that under no circumstances were they to fly through the mushroom cloud. It would contain radioactivity. The pilots now knew why they had been practicing steep, breakaway turns during their training missions.

The plane that was to carry the bomb had been known only as B-29 number 82. The day the bomb was loaded the mission pilot, Paul Tibbets, had his mother's given names "Enola Gay" painted on its fuselage.

*Colonel Paul Tibbets waves from the cockpit
of his B-29 bomber before departing to drop
the Little Boy bomb on Hiroshima.*

The original plan was to have the bomb fully armed at takeoff, but Parsons had seen too many B-29s roll off the runway and catch fire during takeoff. He was afraid that if that happened to the *Enola Gay* it could trigger a nuclear explosion and blow up half the island. He decided that he would arm the bomb after takeoff. Groves, who would have objected to this last minute change in procedure, was cabled of the change only after it was too late for him to do anything about it.

The *Enola Gay* had been flying toward Japan for several hours before the bomb was fully armed. It was only then that Tibbets announced into the intercom, "We are carrying the world's first atomic bomb."

The bomb bay doors to the *Enola Gay* swung open over Hiroshima at 8:15 A.M. local time. Lightened by nearly 10,000 pounds (4,540 kilograms), the plane lurched upward. There was what seemed like a long delay and suddenly a bright light filled the plane. First one shockwave, then another rattled it. Tibbets radioed Tinian with an unemotional message: "Target visually bombed with good results."

The copilot, who was keeping his own notes, wrote, "My God, what have we done?"

That was a question that a lot of Americans asked—but only later. President Truman was still aboard ship coming back from Europe when he got the news. "This is the greatest day in history," he exulted.[2]

Groves phoned Oppenheimer at Los Alamos to tell him the bomb had gone off "with a very big bang indeed." Oppie was not as exultant as Truman, but he was both pleased and happy. When the announcement went out over the intercom system Anne Wilson, Oppie's secretary, recalled,

"The place went up like we'd won the Army-Navy game." When Oppie strode into the auditorium to be greeted by his cheering staff, he clasped his hands above his head in the pose of a winning fighter.

The Japanese quite literally did not know what had hit them. Before they really found out, they were hit again. On August 9 the Fat Man, a plutonium bomb, was dropped over the Japanese city of Nagasaki. And more bombs were in the ready to go. But in Washington it was decided that they might not be necessary. It looked as though Japan were now ready to surrender. On August 15 the emperor of Japan went on the radio to announce that his government had already notified the Allied powers of its surrender. It was the first time the Japanese people ever heard their emperor's voice.

"The enemy has begun to employ a new and most cruel bomb," the emperor said, "the power of which to do damage is indeed incalculable, taking the toll of many innocent lives. Should we continue to fight it would not only result in an ultimate collapse and obliteration of the Japanese nation, but also it would lead to the total extinction of human civilization. . . ."[3]

The war was finally and completely over.

It wasn't until the Hiroshima bombing that the world at large learned of the existence of the atomic bomb. For most Americans it came as wonderful news. It meant the end of a long and ferocious war against a tenacious and hated enemy. In 1945, Americans really *did* remember Pearl Harbor.

When General Groves was admonished by General George C. Marshall against greeting the bombing with "too much gratification" because so many Japanese had been

The city of Hiroshima,
after the bombing

killed, Groves shot back that he was not thinking so much about Japanese casualties "as I was about the men who had made the Bataan death march." After the surrender of Bataan in 1942, as many as 10,000 Philippine and American soldiers died of starvation, disease, beatings, and execution as their Japanese captors marched them from the Bataan Peninsula to prison camps in the north. This was just one of many terrible events in the war which were burned into the consciousness of the American public.[4]

Physicist Richard Feynman had been absolutely euphoric when he witnessed the successful Trinity blast. But after the reality of Hiroshima sank in he became extremely depressed. Sitting in a restaurant on New York's 59th Street, he calculated that an atomic bomb would vaporize buildings as far as 34th Street. When he saw people constructing a bridge he thought they were crazy, because it was now useless to build new things.[5]

Most Americans did not feel that way. Inevitably war creates its own morality. Acts that were unthinkable before the war become accepted as commonplace. The Allies had come to accept saturation bombings of cities and their civilian populations, which in many respects could be as deadly as the atomic bomb itself. To most people the atomic bomb seemed to be just a very big bomb—at first the general public had no idea of how big a nuclear weapon might become. And people did not know about the radiation.

The atomic bomb had been designed as an explosive weapon, not a radiation weapon. The scientists knew that some dangerous radiation would be released in the blast, but the effects of the radiation were far worse than anyone had imagined. Postwar censorship kept many of the details away from the American public for at least a year. And the worst effects of the radiation, the leukemia, the cancer, the genetic damage, did not really show up for several years. The atomic bomb was not just a bigger bomb: it moved warfare into an entirely new and terrible realm.

The Hiroshima bombing became, and remains, one of the most controversial episodes in American history. In 1995 the Smithsonian Institution Air and Space Museum was preparing a major exhibit to mark the 50th anniversary of the bombing and the end of World War II in the Pacific. When details of the exhibit leaked out they ignited a firestorm of protest from veterans' groups and others who felt that the overall tone of the exhibit put too much emphasis on the suffering of the Japanese and made the Americans look like aggressors. Ultimately the plans for the exhibit were scaled back to little more than a display of the fuselage of the *Enola Gay*. The controversy was one of the most heated in the history of the Smithsonian. A plan to put a picture of the mushroom-shaped cloud on a commemorative postage stamp was also abandoned.

In September 1949, President Truman announced that the Soviet Union had tested an atomic bomb. Though it was known that the Soviets were working on nuclear weapons, the timing came as a shock for they had advanced much more quickly than anticipated. The arms race was now on in earnest. The United States began working on the hydrogen bomb—Edward Teller's "super"—a move that Oppenheimer opposed. The Soviets were also hard at work on a hydrogen bomb.

Finally, in 1953, at the height of the Cold War, with a fanatic anti-Communist hysteria, symbolized by Senator Joseph McCarthy of Wisconsin, raging throughout America, J. Robert Oppenheimer's left-wing past, and opposition to the hydrogen bomb, caught up with him.

Oppenheimer, then director of the Institute of Advanced Studies at Princeton, was accused of "more probably than not . . . functioning as an espionage agent." A hearing was convened before a three-man personnel security board of the Atomic Energy Commission on April 12, 1954. The charges were essentially nothing much more than the information that had been known, and rejected, when Oppenheimer became head of Los Alamos.

An impressive number of Oppie's former colleagues testified on his behalf. Groves equivocated. He said that he did not believe that Oppenheimer was a security risk, but that he should not be cleared because security standards had been tightened since the war.

Probably the most powerful witness against Oppenheimer was Edward Teller. Teller was angry that Oppie had never supported his hydrogen bomb. He said that Oppenheimer had shown poor judgment and should not be granted a security clearance. By a vote of 2 to 1 the board agreed. While no finding of disloyalty was made, Oppenheimer was stripped of his security clearance "because of the proof of fundamental defects in his 'character.'"

The man who had probably done more than any other single individual to make the Manhattan Project work—to give America the atomic bomb, was sent back to Princeton under a cloud from which he never really emerged.

In 1963, President Lyndon B. Johnson tried to make amends by granting Oppie the Fermi Award for scientific achievement. Oppenheimer, already gravely ill, told Johnson "it has taken some charity and some courage to make this award. . . ."

Three years later Oppenheimer died of throat cancer. He was nearly a forgotten man.

Chapter 10

THE DOOMSDAY CLOCK

THE NUCLEAR WEAPONS, which had begun with the Manhattan Project, dominated the thinking of humanity for decades.

Everyone knew that the United States and the Soviet Union possessed enough nuclear weapons and the means to deliver them to destroy each other, and perhaps the entire world. During the 1950s, American schoolchildren took part in atomic bomb drills. When the air-raid siren sounded they practiced diving under their desks to protect them from the atomic blast and covering their heads with a jacket or sweater to protect from the radioactive fallout. It was the "duck and cover" strategy.

Throughout the country, public and private shelters were built and stocked with food and other necessities to sustain the occupants for several weeks while the intense radiation from the nuclear attack subsided. Air-raid sirens were tested regularly.

An entire generation grew up believing that nuclear war was probable—and that their generation might be the last generation.

At first the U.S. government had been reluctant to give Leo Szilard $6,000 to carry out some basic research on the possibility of an atomic bomb. In a comprehensive study released in July 1998 by the Brookings Institution, it was estimated that since that first appropriation to Szilard the United States has spent 5.8 trillion dollars on nuclear weapons programs. That is more than on any single program except social security. It was more than welfare payments, interest on the national debt, Medicare, education, veterans benefits—more than practically anything else.

No one knows how much the Soviet Union spent on their nuclear program during this period—but it was almost certainly enough to help bankrupt the country and bring about the fall of Communism, the system that the nuclear weapons had been built to protect.

Stephen Schwartz, who was chairman of the Brookings study, said, "In the end cleanup costs may be as much as the weapons cost in the first place."[1]

For decades both superpowers relied on the theory of Mutual Assured Destruction—MAD—or the Balance of Terror to find ways of avoiding a major military confrontation. And it worked. The feared thermonuclear war between the United States and the Soviet Union did not take place. After 1945 nuclear weapons were never used in a warfare situation, though the fear that they would be cast a huge shadow over the final half of the 20th century.

Many of the scientific veterans of Los Alamos came to the University of Chicago where they began a public affairs science magazine called *The Bulletin of the Atomic Scientists*. Its cover, repeated on each new issue, featured a representation of the hands of a clock nearing midnight. This was the Doomsday Clock. In the beginning the clock was set at 15 minutes to midnight—midnight, of course, being nuclear destruction.

Over the years the setting has varied a good deal. The Doomsday Clock measured the danger as close as two minutes to midnight in 1953 after both the United States and the Soviet Union tested hydrogen bombs. But over time the tensions began to fade as the world seemed to have come to terms with nuclear weapons and learned how to live with them.

Then the Soviet Union itself collapsed and the hair-trigger confrontation between the two major nuclear superpowers came to an end. In 1991 the hands on the Doomsday Clock were changed to 17 minutes to midnight, their safest setting ever. In 1995, 3 minutes were lost to the stalled nuclear arms reduction talks. Then in June 1998 the board of *The Bulletin of the Atomic Scientists* moved the hands forward by another five minutes to 9 before midnight. The primary reason for this change was that a few weeks earlier, first India and then Pakistan tested their own nuclear weapons and became members of the nuclear "club."[2]

At the end of World War II only the United States and Britain possessed the knowledge and technology to produce nuclear weapons. The Soviet Union officially joined the club in 1949, and a few years later so did France and, far more significantly, China. And there matters stood for decades.

Just because a nation didn't test its own nuclear weapons or officially announce that it had a nuclear arsenal did not mean it had no interest in such weapons. A lot of other countries were trying to develop their own nuclear weapons, and a number had actually done so. Israel's nuclear weapons program is one of the worst kept secrets in his-

Leonard Rieser, chairman of the board of The Bulletin of the Atomic Scientists, *resets the hands of the Doomsday Clock after India and Pakistan prove they have nuclear capabilities.*

tory. Everybody knows that the Israelis have a nuclear arsenal, they just won't admit it or publicly tip their hand by testing weapons in a way that the tests can be detected. A number of other countries were also reliably reported to possess nuclear arsenals. They just wouldn't admit it either.

Then in May 1998, India carried out a series of nuclear tests, and in this dramatic fashion announced that it too had joined the nuclear club. India was known to have an advanced nuclear program, but the tests still came as a shock. India was the land of Mohandas Gandhi, the century's chief proponent of nonviolence. Even though a newly elected Hindu nationalist government had announced its intention of developing a nuclear arsenal, the timing of the tests had completely fooled the CIA, which is supposed to monitor such activities.

India's neighbor, and deadly rival, Pakistan, followed suit with its own series of nuclear tests just a few weeks later. Like India, Pakistan was known to have an extensive nuclear program. Until 1998 it just hadn't taken the public step of testing its weapons.

Suddenly the arms race was back in a new and very dangerous way. In the past half century India and Pakistan have fought four wars, which settled none of the many disputes between them. The next war might be fought with nuclear weapons. Some military analysts believe that the tensions and hatreds between the two countries are so great that the world is closer to a nuclear war than at any time since the depths of the Cold War.

What was most striking was the reaction of the people in the two countries. Polls taken in India shortly after the tests, and after practically every other country in the world condemned the testing, showed that almost 90 percent of the Indian population favored the nuclear tests. In Pakistan there was dancing in the streets after the Pakistani tests were announced. It was the same sort of reaction that the American people had when they first found out about the American atomic bomb.

Both India and Pakistan are poor countries that can ill afford the enormous expense of a nuclear weapons program. Yet both countries passionately believe that such weapons are absolutely essential for their security, and they give the countries a great sense of national pride. Now they too are members of the nuclear club and that makes them world powers that can command international respect. Any country that aspires to be a world power or feels gravely threatened by a traditional enemy may now feel that a nuclear arsenal is essential. The materials and technology needed to build nuclear weapons and the means of delivering them are more widely available than ever before.

It is assumed that Israel has nuclear weapons, though the government has never acknowledged this. Other countries (North Korea, Iran, and Libya) are known or believed to have nuclear weapons programs. Iraq had an active nuclear weapons development program, but it was disrupted first by an Israeli attack and later by the Gulf War. South Africa and Brazil have given up their attempts to build their own atomic bombs.

International efforts to control the spread of nuclear weapons technology and materials are feeble and nonproliferation treaties have bogged down, even in the United States.

Looking back we can now see that the Manhattan Project was one of the most significant events of the 20th century. At the end of the century and the beginning of a new millennium, the forces unleashed at Trinity on July 16, 1945, still pose what may be the greatest threat to the continued survival of our species.

Chronology

1939   The Hungarian Conspiracy persuades Albert Einstein to write a letter to President Franklin D. Roosevelt about the possibility of an atomic bomb (July 16).
Alexander Sachs meets Roosevelt to deliver Einstein's letter (October 11).
Advisory Committee on Uranium set up (late fall).

1940   Funds for building graphite-uranium system for creating nuclear chain reaction appropriated.

1941   Pearl Harbor bombed. The United States enters the war (December 7).

1942   General Leslie Groves put in overall charge of the Manhattan Project (September 17).
Groves appoints J. Robert Oppenheimer scientific director (October).
Los Alamos, New Mexico, chosen as site for primary research facility (November 16).
University of Chicago team led by Enrico Fermi creates first self-sustaining chain reaction (December 2).

1943   Successful sabotage of German-controlled heavy-water plant in Norway (February 27).

1943   Los Alamos officially opens (April 15).
Work begins on developing implosion method for plutonium bomb (summer).
Oak Ridge, Tennessee, nuclear plant opens (August).
Construction begins at Hanford, Washington, facility (fall).
Norwegian heavy-water plant bombed (November 16).

1944   Ferry carrying heavy water from Norway to Germany sunk (February).
Construction begins at Trinity nuclear test site (November).
Plot to assassinate Werner Heisenberg (December).

1945   Alsos unit captures the majority of German atomic scientists (April).
President Roosevelt dies. Harry Truman becomes president and learns of Manhattan Project (April 12).
Germany surrenders (May 8).
"Big Three" meet in Potsdam (July 15).
Successful test of plutonium bomb at Trinity site (July 16).
President Truman issues Potsdam Declaration calling for Japan's unconditional surrender and warning of "utter destruction." Material for making atomic bomb arrives at Tinian (July 26).
Atomic bomb dropped on Hiroshima (August 6).
Atomic bomb dropped on Nagasaki (August 9).
Japan makes offer of surrender (August 10).
Surrender offer accepted (August 14).

1949   Soviet Union develops nuclear capability.

Notes

Introduction

1. Richard Rhodes, *The Making of the Atomic Bomb* (New York: Simon & Schuster, 1986) p. 672.
2. Ibid., p. 673.
3. Ferenc M. Szasz, *The Day the Sun Rose Twice* (Albuquerque: University of New Mexico Press, 1984) p. 85.

Chapter 1

1. Dan Kurzman, *The Day of the Bomb: Countdown to Hiroshima* (New York: McGraw-Hill, 1986) p. 25.
2. Peter Wyden, *Day One: Before Hiroshima and After* (New York: Simon & Schuster, 1984) p. 37.

Chapter 2

1. Rhodes, p. 433.
2. At the time the author, then a seven-year-old, lived about four blocks from where the experiment was carried out. No one in the neighborhood had the faintest notion of what was going on in Stagg Field that day. Like most people he first learned of the event several years after

the war ended from a rather sensationalized film called
The Beginning or the End.
3. Rhodes, p. 437.
4. Ibid., p. 440.
5. Wyden, p. 54.

Chapter 3
1. Rhodes, p. 426.
2. Ibid., p. 449.
3. Ibid., pp. 448–449.
4. Wyden, p. 67.

Chapter 4
1. Wyden, p. 95.
2. Kurzman, p. 160.
3. Ibid., p. 181.

Chapter 5
1. Rhodes, p. 456.
2. Ibid., p. 514.
3. Ibid., p. 517.
4. Thomas Powers, *Heisenberg's War: The Secret History of the German Bomb* (New York: Knopf, 1993) p. 399.

Chapter 6
1. Szasz, p. 31.
2. Ibid., p. 59.
3. Wyden, p. 115.
4. Rhodes, pp. 613–614.

Chapter 7
1. Szasz, p. 69.
2. Wyden, p. 115.

3. Rhodes, p. 657.
4. Szasz, pp. 85–86.

Chapter 8
1. Kurzman, p. 54.
2. Joseph Albright and Marcia Kunstel, *Bombshell: The Secret Story of Ted Hall* (New York: Random House, 1997) pp. 94–95.
3. Ibid., p. 152.
4. Ibid., p. 194.
5. Ibid., p. 289.
6. Ibid., pp. 283–284.

Chapter 9
1. Wyden, pp. 226–227.
2. Ibid., p. 289.
3. Ibid., p. 305.
4. Ibid., p. 287.
5. Ibid., p. 215.

Chapter 10
1. *The Washington Post,* July 1, 1998, p. 2.
2. Richard Parker, Knight Ridder News Service, June 11, 1998.

Bibliography

Albright, Joseph, and Marcia Kunstel. *Bombshell: The Secret Story of Ted Hall*. New York: Random House, 1997.

Alperovitz, Gar. *The Decision to Use the Atomic Bomb*. New York: Vintage Books, 1996.

Gallagher, Thomas M. *Assault on Norway: Sabotaging the Nazi Bomb*. New York: Harcourt, Brace, Jovanovich, 1975.

Groueff, Stephanie. *Manhattan Project: The Untold Story of Making the Atomic Bomb*. Boston: Little Brown, 1967.

Groves, Leslie. *Now It Can Be Told: The Story of the Manhattan Project*. New York: Harper & Row, 1962.

Harper, Stephen. *The Miracle of Deliverance: The Case for the Bombing of Hiroshima and Nagasaki*. New York: Stein & Day, 1986.

Hersey, John. *Hiroshima* (new edition). New York: Vintage Books, 1989.

Kanon, Joseph. *Los Alamos: A Novel*. New York: Broadway Books, 1997.

Kunetka, James W. *City of Fire: Los Alamos and the Birth of the Atomic Age 1943–1945*. Albuquerque: University of New Mexico Press, 1979.

———. *Oppenheimer: The Years of Risk*. Englewood Cliffs, NJ: Prentice Hall, 1982.

Kurzman, Dan. *The Day of the Bomb: Countdown to Hiroshima*. New York: McGraw-Hill, 1986.

Lanouette, William, with Bela Szilard. *Genius in the Shadows: A Biography of Leo Szilard*. New York: Maxwell, Macmillan International, 1992.

Laurence, William L. *Dawn Over Zero: The Story of the Atomic Bomb*. New York: Knopf, 1946.

Lifton, Robert J. *Hiroshima in America: Fifty Years of Denial*. New York: Putnam, 1995.

McPherson, Malcolm. *Timebomb: Fermi, Heisenberg and the Race for the Atomic Bomb*. New York: Dutton, 1986.

Powers, Thomas. *Heisenberg's War: The Secret History of the German Bomb*. New York: Knopf, 1993.

Rhodes, Richard. *Dark Sun: The Making of the Hydrogen Bomb*. New York: Simon & Schuster, 1995.

———. *The Making of the Atomic Bomb*. New York: Simon & Schuster, 1986.

Sanger, Stephen L. *Working on the Bomb: An Oral History of WWII*. Portland, OR: Continuing Education Press, Portland State University, 1995.

Smith, Alice Kimball, and Charles Weiner (eds). *Robert Oppenheimer, Letters and Recollections*. Cambridge, MA: Harvard University Press, 1980.

Snow, C.P. *The Physicists*. Boston: Little Brown, 1981.

Stein, R. Conrad. *The Manhattan Project*. Chicago: Children's Press, 1993.

Stern, Philip M. *The Oppenheimer Case: Security on Trial.* New York: Harper & Row, 1969.

Sweeney, Charles W. *War's End: An Eyewitness Account of America's Last Atomic Mission.* New York: Avon Books, 1997.

Szasz, Ferenc M. *The Day the Sun Rose Twice.* Albuquerque: University of New Mexico Press, 1984.

Wyden, Peter. *Day One: Before Hiroshima and After.* New York: Simon & Schuster, 1984.

Index

Page numbers in *italics* refer to illustrations.

Abel, Rudolf, 96
Acton, Lord, 18
Advisory Committee on Uranium, 20–22
Alamogordo Bombing Range (Trinity site)
    atomic bomb test at, 9–11, 74–75, *76*, 77–78, *79*, 80, *81*, 82, 102
    construction of, 65
Albright, Joseph, 98
Allison, Sam, 78
Alsos (intelligence unit), 60
Anderson, Herbert L., 53
Anta and Aden, 96
Anti-Communism, 90, 108–109
Atom, splitting, 13–15
Atomic bomb
    dropped on Japan, 95, 99–102, 104–105, *106*, 107–108
    spies and, 84–88, 90–92, 94–98
    test at Trinity, 9–11, 74–75, *76*, 77–78, *79*, 80, *81*, 82, 102
Atomic energy, 67–69, 83

Bainbridge, Kenneth T., 80
Bataan death march, 107
Berg, Morris (Moe), 58–60, *59*
Bethe, Hans, 43
Bohr, Niels, 12, 13, 57–58, 66–69, *68*, 87
Bothe, Walter, 53
Briggs, Lyman J., 21
Brookings Institution, 111
Bulletin of the Atomic Scientists, The, 111, 112
Byrnes, James F. "Jimmy," 72, 73

Cadmium, 27, 28
Carbon, 52–53
Churchill, Winston, 64, 67–69, 73, 82, 83, 100, 102

CIA (Central Intelligence Agency), 58, *93*, 114
Cohen, Lona, 95
Columbia University, 24, 38, 53, 87
Communists, 36, 85–86, 92
Compton, Arthur Holly, 47
Condon, Edward U., 49

D Day invasion, 68
Deuterium, 52
Doomsday Clock, 111–112, *113*
Dunkirk, 22

Einstein, Albert, 13–16, *17*, 18, 19, 67
Eisenhower, Dwight D., 72
Enola Gay (airplane), 102, *103*, 104, 108

Fascism, 14, 86
Fat Man (bomb), 64, 101, 105
FBI (Federal Bureau of Investigation), 36, 88, 97
Fermi, Enrico, 10, 21, 24, 25, 27–29, 43, 44, *45*, 53, 95, 96
Fermi, Laura, 10
Fermi Award, 109
Feynman, Richard, *45*, 49, 51, 107
Franco, Francisco, 86
Frisch, Otto, 23
Fuchs, Klaus, 86–88, 90, *91*, 92, 94
Fulton, Robert, 18–19

German bomb project, 52–62
Gold, Harry, 87, 88
Graphite, 24, 25, *26*, 27, 53
Great Depression, 36, 71, 85
Green, Georgia, 11
Greenglass, David, 88
Groves, Leslie Richard, 11, 30–34, *32*, 63, 64, *81*, 102, 104, 109
  compared to Oppenheimer, 34–35
  German bomb project and, 53, 55, 57, 58, 60
  as head of Manhattan Project, 30–36, 44, 49, 74, 77, 78
  relations with Oppenheimer, 37–39

Hall, Ted, 91–92, *93*, 94–98
Hanford, Washington, 63, 74
Heavy water, 52–58
Heisenberg, Werner, 23–24, 57–61
Hiroshima, 100, 101, 104–105, *106*, 107–108
Hitler, Adolf, 15, 16, 22, 24, 36, 57, 61, 73, 85, 86
Hydrogen bomb, 47, 108, 109, 112

Implosion method, 46, 64, 66
India, 112–115
Israel, 112–113

Johnson, Lyndon B., 109

Jornada del Muerto site, 64–65

Jumbo, 65–66

Kapitza, Peter, 69
Kistiakowsky, George, 77, 78
Kunstel, Marcia, 98
Kurchatov, Igor, 90
Kurnakov, Sergi, 92, 94

Laurence, William, 77
Lawrence, Ernest, 33, 35, 37
Little Boy (bomb), 64, 101
Los Alamos, *43* (*see also* Alamogordo Bombing Range)
    accommodations at, 48
    opening of, 44
    organizational chart of, 48
    search for, 40–42, *43*
    security at, 49, 51
    weekly meetings at, *45*

Marshall, George C., 105
McCarthy, Joseph, 108
Mutual Assured Destruction (MAD), 111

Nagasaki, 100, 105
Napoléon Bonaparte, 18
Nazism, 14, 86
Neddermeyer, Seth, 46, 64
Nuclear chain reaction, 21, 24–25, *26*, 27–29, 53
Nuclear fission, 13–15

Oak Ridge, Tennessee, 63, 69
O'Keefe, Bernard J., 67
Oppenheimer, J. Robert, 33, *35*, *45*, 63, 74, 78, *81*, 102 (*see also* Atomic bomb)
    compared to Groves, 34–35
    death of, 109
    hydrogen bomb and, 108, 109
    implosion theory and, 46
    politics of, 36
    recruitment of scientists and, 42–43
    relations with Groves, 37–39
    Roosevelt's death and, 70
    stripped of security clearance, 109
    work schedule of, 66
OSS (Office of Special Services), 58

Pakistan, 112–115
Parsons, William "Deke," 102, 104
Pash, Boris T., 60, 61
Patton, George, 64
Pearl Harbor, 24, 105
Peierls, Rudolf, 23, 69
Plutonium, 46, 63, 74
Potsdam Conference, 82–83
Potsdam Declaration, 100, 101
Powers, Thomas, 60

Rabi, Isidore I., 9–10, 36, 43
Rhodes, Richard, 25
Rieser, Leonard, *113*
Roentgen, Wilhelm, 13
Roosevelt, Eleanor, 75
Roosevelt, Franklin D., 15,
    16, 18–19, 64, 67–72
Rosenberg, Ethel, 88, *89*, 90,
    97
Rosenberg, Julius, 88, *89*,
    90, 92, 97
Rutherford, Ernest, 13

Sachs, Alexander, 16, 18–19
Sax, Saville, 92, *93*, 94, 96,
    97
Schwartz, Stephen, 111
Segre, Emilio, 10
Spanish Civil War, 86
Spies, 84–88, 90–92, 94–98
Stagg Field site, 24–25, 27–
    29, 95–96
Stalin, Joseph, 57, 67, 68,
    73, 83, 85, 86, 100
Stimson, Henry W., 71
Szilard, Leo, 15–16, *17*, 18–
    22, 24, 29, 44, 111

Teller, Edward, 15, 20, 43,
    47, 51, 95, 108, 109

Theoretical physics, 13–14
Tibbets, Paul, 102, *103*,
    104
Tinian Island, 99–102
Trinity site (*see* Alamogordo
    Bombing Range)
Truman, Harry S, 71–73,
    82–83, 95, 100–102, 104,
    108

Ulam, Stanislaw M., 67
U.S.S. *Indianapolis*, 101
University of Chicago, 24–
    25, 27–29, 38, 53, 95,
    111
Uranium, 23, 24, 27, 45, 52,
    63, 69, 101

V-1 and V-2 rockets, 61
V-E Day, 73
Vemork plant, Norway, 53–
    55
Von Neumann, John, 46–47

Weil, George, 27, 28
Wieselman, Mrs. H.W., 11
Wigner, Eugene, 15–16, 18,
    20, 29
Wilson, Anne, 104
Winchester Company, 50